Learning
Stories in
Practice

Sara Miller McCune founded SAGE Publishing in 1965 to support the dissemination of usable knowledge and educate a global community. SAGE publishes more than 1000 journals and over 800 new books each year, spanning a wide range of subject areas. Our growing selection of library products includes archives, data, case studies and video. SAGE remains majority owned by our founder and after her lifetime will become owned by a charitable trust that secures the company's continued independence.

Los Angeles | London | New Delhi | Singapore | Washington DC | Melbourne

Learning
Stories in
Practice

Margaret Carr
and
Wendy Lee

Los Angeles | London | New Delhi
Singapore | Washington DC | Melbourne

Los Angeles | London | New Delhi
Singapore | Washington DC | Melbourne

SAGE Publications Ltd
1 Oliver's Yard
55 City Road
London EC1Y 1SP

SAGE Publications Inc.
2455 Teller Road
Thousand Oaks, California 91320

SAGE Publications India Pvt Ltd
B 1/I 1 Mohan Cooperative Industrial Area
Mathura Road
New Delhi 110 044

SAGE Publications Asia-Pacific Pte Ltd
3 Church Street
#10-04 Samsung Hub
Singapore 049483

© Margaret Carr and Wendy Lee, 2019

First published 2019

Editor: Jude Bowen
Assistant editor: Catriona McMullen
Production editor: Nicola Carrier
Copyeditor: Gemma Marren
Proofreader: Derek Markham
Indexer: Cathy Heath
Marketing manager: Dilhara Attygalle
Cover design: Wendy Scott
Typeset by: C&M Digitals (P) Ltd, Chennai, India
Printed in the Great Britain by Bell & Bain Ltd, Glasgow

Library of Congress Control Number: 2018966109

British Library Cataloguing in Publication data

A catalogue record for this book is available from the British Library

ISBN 978-1-5264-2374-0
ISBN 978-1-5264-2375-7 (pbk)

At SAGE we take sustainability seriously. Most of our products are printed in the UK using responsibly sourced papers and boards. When we print overseas we ensure sustainable papers are used as measured by the PREPS grading system. We undertake an annual audit to monitor our sustainability.

Contents

List of Learning Stories

About the Authors

Margaret Carr is a Professor of Education at the Wilf Malcolm Institute of Educational Research at the University of Waikato, in Hamilton, New Zealand. Before she joined the Faculty of Education at Waikato, she was a geographer at Victoria University in Wellington, New Zealand, where there was a strong focus by the professors on social and cultural change. This formed a background for her interest in the role of education in society, and in Hamilton she gained a qualification in early childhood education and worked as a kindergarten teacher before becoming a lecturer in education at the university. Her PhD thesis was entitled 'Technological Practice in Early Childhood as a Dispositional Milieu'. New Zealand has provided a number of opportunities for professors to research *with* early childhood teachers on topics chosen by the teachers, and Margaret has frequently published with teachers. Learning Stories as an assessment practice was developed for the 1996 *Te Whāriki* bicultural curriculum (later revised in 2017); the development of narrative assessment is told in the 2001 Sage book, *Assessment in Early Childhood Settings: Learning Stories*, and further developed in the 2012 Sage book, *Learning Stories: Constructing Learner Identities in Early Education*. The latter book was co-authored with Wendy Lee, and this partnership has combined academic and professional wisdom in many publications and presentations over many years.

Wendy Lee is the director of Educational Leadership Project (ELP) Ltd, which provides professional learning for teachers in the Early Childhood Education (ECE) sector in New Zealand and in other countries. Wendy started her career as a kindergarten teacher before becoming a lecturer in ECE at the North Shore Teachers Training College, Auckland. Her passion for ECE resulted in her becoming national President of the Kindergarten Teachers Association and then, as a parent, her strong advocacy for the rights of parents and children in society led to community work and ultimately to her role as a Councillor for the Rotorua District Council. Wendy's strong belief in life-long education, social equity and the key role of the ECE sector in achieving this, led to collaboration with Professor Margaret Carr over a range of ECE research projects emanating from Te Whāriki. These included co-directorship of the National ECE Assessment and Learning Exemplar project resulting in the Kei Tua o te Pae books on assessment. Her determination to provide all ECE teachers with practical tools that are deeply embedded in the principles of Te Whāriki is reflected in the development and application of Learning Stories for both assessment and professional learning. This focus has resulted in a growing, global interest in the application and adoption of Learning Stories, some of which are included in this book.

Acknowledgements

Acknowledgements and gratitude to the many early childhood practitioners who sent us so many wonderful Learning Stories. We regret that we could not include them all.

ABC Educare, NZ

Albany Kindergarten, NZ

Bear Park, NZ

Beverton Preschool, Ireland

Cambridge Road Community Kindergarten, NZ

Campus Creche Trust, NZ

Chelsea Kindergarten, NZ

Child Development Resources, USA

Cowgate Under 5s Centre, Scotland

DBICC Jigsaw Centre, Ireland

Educare Kensington, NZ

Ferndale Kindergarte, NZ

Greerton Early Learning Centre, NZ

Guiyang City Central Experimental Kindergarten, China

Guiyang Liuyi Kindergarten, China

Haeata Community Campus, NZ

Haike Kindergarten, Chengdu, China

Hainault House, Early Childhood Ireland

Halifax St Children's Centre, Australia

Happy Days Ballyporeen, Ireland

HomeCare, USA

Intercultural Child and Family Centre, Canada

Kentstown Montessori, Ireland

Kidsfirst Diamond Harbour, NZ

Las Americas Children's Center, USA

Learn and Play Family Child Care, USA

Lincoln University Childcare, NZ

Lintotts Community Childcare Centre, NZ

Little One's Garden, NZ

Lixin Old Town Central Kindergarten, China

Mana Tamariki, NZ

Mangere Bridge Kindergarten, NZ

Miyamai Kindergarten, Japan

Naíonra na nÓg, Ireland

North Beach Community Preschool, NZ

Orfalea Family Children's Centre, USA

Pacific Primary, USA

Parkland School Division, USA

Pennington Kindergarten, Australia

Prescott Learning Centre, Canada

Roskill South Kindergarten, NZ

Sanyili No. 1 Kindergarten, China

Selwyn Kindergarten, NZ

Shanglin Kindergarten
Chongqing, China

Shenzhen Experimental
Kindergarten, China

Side by Side Early Childhood
Consultation, USA

Stony Plain Central School, Canada

Storyteller Children's Center, USA

Te Whare Manaaki Kindergarten, NZ

The Kindergarten of Changsha
Education Bureau, China

The No. 1 Kindergarten of Baiyun
District, China

The No. 1 Kindergarten of
Yinchuan, China

The No. 16 Kindergarten of
Chengdu, China

The No. 2 Kindergarten of Daxing
District, China

The No. 8 Kindergarten of
Guiyang, China

The Purple Penquin
Creche, Ireland

Transition House, USA

Tumuaki Ki Mua Lady May, NZ

Westlake Forrest Hill
Kindergarten, NZ

Whaihanga Early
Learning Centre, NZ

Yandunlu Kindergarten, China

Many thanks to Claire Chapman for her valuable support during the preparation of the book.

The authors and the publisher are grateful for permission to reproduce the following material in this book:

Images of the book We're Going on a Bear Hunt by Michael Rosen and illustrated by Helen Oxenbury, used in Learning Story 4.4 My learner identity. Text © 1998 Michael Rosen. Illustrations © 1989 Helen Oxenbury. Reproduced by permission of Walker Books Ltd, www.walker.co.uk.

Images of the book Flutterby Butterfly, Where Did You Come From?, used in Learning Story 6.9 Purerehua butterfly. Reproduced by permission of Peter Edward Smith, Educational Solutions Ltd.

1

Introduction

Throughout the ages and across cultures story continues to express the fundamental nature of humanity. Stories are not to be treated lightly as they both carry, and inspire, significant obligations and responsibilities: stories must be cared for as they are at the heart of how we make meaning of our experience of the world. (Janice Huber, Vera Caine, Marilyn Huber and Pam Steeves, 2016: 214)

> # Key messages
>
> - The power of stories
> - Continuing a conversation about a dispositional theory of learning
> - Funds of learning disposition
> - Assessment for learning in early years or early childhood education: the purpose and structure of this book

The power of stories

The viewpoint of Janice Huber and the others named on the title page of this chapter is also the view in this book. It is that: *stories* of teaching and learning are at the heart of how we make meaning of our experiences. The classic storyteller about the power of stories is Jerome Bruner; his writing about education and development in terms of language, learning and narrative has inspired many of the ideas in this book. In Chapter 4 of his book *Making Stories* he asks 'So why narrative?', and responds to his own question (2003: 89, 93):

> One truth is surely self-evident: for all that narrative is one of our evident delights, it is serious business. For better or worse, it is our preferred, perhaps even our obligatory medium for expressing human aspirations and their vicissitudes, our own and those of others. Our stories also impose a structure, a compelling reality on what we experience, even a philosophical stance.
>
> Through narrative, we construct, reconstruct, in some ways reinvent yesterday and tomorrow. Memory and imagination fuse the process.

Vivian Gussin Paley writes about the *children's* stories in her classrooms. Her many books document the stories told by children, written down by teachers, and acted out by the children. In her 2004 book *A Child's Work: The Importance of Fantasy Play* she states that:

> If fantasy play provides the nourishing habitat for the growth of cognitive, narrative, and social connectivity in young children, then it is surely the staging area for our common enterprise: an early school experience that best represents the natural development of young children. (2004: 8)

Perhaps Learning Stories are a combination of the teachers' stories about their children's stories; often teachers will ask the children's advice, and certainly they will have a curriculum in mind. But they will be stories, and they will pay attention to 'Making Learning Whole' as David Perkins argues in his book with that name. The power of Learning Stories is not restricted to the early childhood sector. It is increasingly being adopted in the primary sector and Bevan Holloway, a secondary school teacher, says in his paper on assessment and play (Holloway,

2018: 39), 'Learning Stories made me notice the front end of the curriculum in a way I hadn't before, giving me an authentic way to acknowledge students exhibiting those "soft" skills'.

Continuing a conversation about assessment and dispositional theory of learning

Bruner and Paley also inspired two earlier books on Learning Stories (Carr, 2001; Carr and Lee, 2012). *Assessment in Early Childhood Settings: Learning Stories* (Carr, 2001: 4–11) argues for a shift in outcomes from skills and knowledges to learning dispositions, and the development of Learning Stories is told in *Learning Stories: Constructing Learner Identities in Early Education* (Carr and Lee, 2012: 34–40). A reason for this book was to finish a conversation that began towards the end of our 2012 book on Learning Stories, where we used the term 'Stores' to refer to 'the intermingling of stores of knowledge and stores of disposition' (Carr and Lee, 2012: 130), and in note 4 at the end of the first chapter in that book, we acknowledged the significant introduction to the literature of the expression 'funds of knowledge' by Norma Gonzàlez, Luis Moll and Cathy Amanti (2005). This expression referred to 'historically accumulated and culturally developed bodies of knowledge and skills essential for household or individual functioning and well-being' (Moll et al., 1992: 133). For the children and families in an early childhood centre or a school classroom these household funds of cultural and community knowledge meet the funds of knowledge (both informal and the formal, espoused and hidden) in the curriculum. In the 2005 book *Funds of Knowledge*, Norma Gonzàlez writes about the *hybridity* that emerges from the intersection of these diverse funds of knowledge. She argues that it is with a 'mutually respectful dialog' that 'we can cross the constructions of difference' (2005: 44). We agree. The viewpoint in this book is that assessment practices like Learning Stories can cross boundaries via assessment portfolios to begin conversations about learning between teachers and children, children and children, teachers and families, children and families. These conversations and the revisiting of Learning Stories with adults and other children build, celebrate and critique the children's growing funds of learning disposition.

Funds of learning disposition

In our 2012 Learning Story book, we chose the term 'stores of disposition' rather than 'funds of disposition', and we set them beside 'stores of knowledge' having reminded the readers of the significant work on social and cultural funds of knowledge by Moll, Amanti, Neff and Gonzàlez (1992), and Gonzàlez, Moll and Amanti (2005). However, in this book we have entitled them *funds of learning disposition*. Developments in early childhood and school contexts of Learning

Stories and learning dispositions have convinced us of the sociocultural parallel of funds of knowledge with funds of learning disposition. In 2016, Bronwen Cowie and Margaret Carr contributed a chapter to an *Encyclopedia of Educational Philosophy and Theory* that set out the possibilities that narrative assessment offers in documenting, supporting and reporting the breadth of children's learning. That chapter is titled: 'Narrative assessment: a sociocultural view'. It discusses the implication of a sociocultural understanding of assessment through a focus on three points:

> (i) narrative assessment as a way of acknowledging the distributed nature of learning, (ii) narrative assessments as improvable objects and opportunities for developing a learning journey, and (iii) narrative assessments as boundary-crossing objects that mediate conversations across interested communities. (2016: 397)

The first point acknowledged that 'learning is entangled with, and made possible through, the material, social, cultural, and historical features of the context for learning'. Children are sensitive to the opportunities to learn, and these features are designed to encourage children to be ready and willing to engage with the opportunities in this place (the topic of Chapters 2 and 3). The second point is about boundary-crossing from one community (the early childhood centre or the school) to another (the home); it is the topic of Chapter 7. The third point is about progress over time (Chapter 8). We return to the notion of learning as a 'tangle' in Chapter 8.

In the 2001 Learning Stories book we explained our assessment frame as children being 'ready, willing and able' to learn. We acknowledge our debt to Lauren Resnick (1987) and to David Perkins, Eileen Jay and Shari Tishman at Harvard (Perkins et al., 1993) for their paper entitled 'Beyond abilities: a dispositional theory of thinking'. In that paper, thinking dispositions are described as having three parts: ability, inclination and sensitivity to occasion. We had adopted this triangle to refer more broadly to learning. These three dimensions overlap, but *inclination* includes the notion of a preferred and positive attitude towards this opportunity to learn something; *sensitivity to occasion* includes a 'reading' of the environment or the culture of the classroom (for example, whether the environment encourages curiosity and exploration; who will be chosen; whether expressing uncertainty or critique is OK), and *ability* includes having at least some of the skills and knowledge needed to approach and to learn this 'something'. These three aspects of a learning disposition have been translated as 'being ready, willing and able' (Carr and Claxton, 1989); this book has more to say about a learning disposition, and we include many Learning Stories that illustrate this in practice. Here is a quote (abridged) from Gary, a primary school principal, talking to researchers during a research project on key competencies, assessment and Learning Stories. The five school key competencies are dispositional 'capabilities for living and lifelong learning'.

We need to make a mind shift in terms of how we go about assessing Key Competencies. You can't tick off 'I'm a caring citizen', 'I participate and contribute'. That form of assessment doesn't sit comfortably cos these are dispositions that we are developing throughout our lives. ... So teachers need to make that shift from the tick box mentality. What's a better way? How can I show development and growth in the Key Competencies? ... How am I going to show that children are reflecting on their learning? Learning Stories have the ability to do that in a very powerful way. (Davis et al., 2013: 19)

Guy Claxton, Meryl Chambers, Graham Powell and Bill Lucas (2011) write about split-screen and dual-focus lesson design. On the one hand the focus is on content or subject area (or the learning area). On the other hand the focus is on learning dispositions (the key competencies). They argue that:

All lessons have a dual purpose, irrespective of the age and ability of young people or the subject area being taught. There is the content dimension, with some material being mastered; and there is the 'epistemic dimension', with some learning skills and habits being exercised. The risk in conventional classrooms ... is that students can be learning habits of compliance and dependence, rather than curiosity and self-reliance. Where teachers are making conscious choices about what habits they will introduce and stretch in the course of the lesson, we call that split-screen, or dual-focus, lesson design. (Claxton et al., 2011: 93)

In the Claxton et al. book, there are graphs that represent data over time from when teachers in seven primary and nine secondary schools began to focus more on 'building learning power' or 'learning habits'. During this same period their test (SATs or GCSE) scores improved – often significantly.

Assessment for learning in early years: early childhood education and school. The purpose and structure of this book

We have often been asked for a follow-on or companion to the 2012 book: one that provides practical advice for teachers who are embarking on a 'narrative assessments-for-learning' journey. So, here, influenced by our ongoing work with teachers across many countries and consistent with the companion 2012 book, is our list of characteristics of assessment that promote learning in early childhood settings or schools with particular emphasis on implementing Learning Stories. Most of our examples are from early childhood centres for children before school, but a number of schools use Learning Stories as well. In both the sectors the principles of assessment for learning are the same, and we explore them in this book using examples from teachers across the world.[1]

This book also encourages discussions about the key features of narrative assessments and the portfolios that we describe as *assessment for learning*. The chapters have developed from the thoughtful comments and questions that teachers have asked us during conversations at conferences, lectures and professional development programmes, and during our research. We have turned these conversations with teachers and students into key ideas, and they frame up this book.

Another implication of these conversations is that teachers in early childhood environments already give feedback to children in order to encourage their learning. This feedback includes gestures, smiles, frowns, laughter, body stance, and nods. In this book, we want to include Learning Stories as 'reified' feedback

(made into a thing, an object; in this case, written down, and maybe photographed). We will discuss some of the ways in which this reification works, while at the same time providing ideas that may answer some of the key questions that have concerned teachers. Each chapter title is a quick reply to the 'teachers' question' that is the subject of that chapter.

Learning Stories are formative assessments. They are not summative in intent, although they may include summative elements. The question to be answered is: 'Are Learning Stories *really* assessments?' This is the discussion in Chapter 2: **Being Formative**.

Narrative assessments focus holistically on *learning dispositions*: being 'ready, willing and able'. The question to be answered is: 'Is there a key feature of Learning Stories assessments that tests can't do?' Assessment for learning will focus not just on knowledge and abilities; the learning will be determined by the characteristics of on-going features that wrap around (are woven with) abilities: inclination and sensitivity to occasion. If the learning environment does not enable the knowledge and ability to flourish, then the assessment is not fair, because the learner will not be *willing* to participate. And if the learning environment or tasks available do not encourage *inclination* – an emotional response, revealed as vital by neuroscientists interested in learning – then the teachers are wasting their time. This is the topic of Chapter 3: **Being Fair**.

The assessments *will be embedded in a clear view of the aims of teaching and learning*. The question here is: 'What do we look for when we write a

Learning Story?' These are the powerful
frameworks or Big Picture learning that we
want for our youngest learners. The connection between the big picture and the
parts (the events that the Learning Story is
about) will need to be recognised by all the
authors and audiences. Usually this will be
enshrined in a national curriculum. In
Chapter 4 we have called it **Recognising
Powerful Frameworks**.

A question to also be answered here is
'Children are at play much of the time: is it
OK to be uncertain about what's going on?'
We appreciate this: both of us (Margaret
and Wendy) have been early years teachers. As a collective, teachers in any one site
will need some time together to constantly
work towards a culture, a climate, where
formative assessment is the 'home language' and the 'next steps' for the learning
will feature in the children's portfolios.
Team teaching and meetings are a significant feature of maximising a collective
climate. Because of the nature of dispositional learning, and the frequently mercurial
nature of children's responses and interests, a teacher's disposition to *manage
ambiguity* is a major requirement. This is
the topic of Chapter 5: **Managing
Ambiguity**.

Encouraging the children to assess their
own learning achievements and strategies
can begin early: 'Can we do this as part of
their Learning Story portfolio? Do we have
to teach differently?' This includes helping
them to notice and recognise that what they
are doing is an example or an opportunity
that connects with the framing in the cur-

riculum. This is about revisiting the portfolio and the Learning Stories. Teachers
have wondered what is the best way to do this. Chapter 6: **Sharing Responsibility
with the Learners** is about these questions.

An implication of topics in Chapters 5 and 6 is the common notion that 'it
takes a village to raise a child'.[2] Assessment for learning in the early years
requires a partnership with families, others in community support roles and
the teachers at the local school. The teacher question is: 'How do we encourage

families to read, and respond to, the stories?' Some of the opportunities for Learning Stories to contribute to developing partnerships with families and community are canvassed in Chapter 7: **Developing Partnerships with Families**.

A portfolio of Learning Stories will recognise, construct, and record the growth of learner identities. Teachers often ask 'How do we describe progress?'. Chapter 8: **Constructing Progress** reviews the ways that progress has been described in Learning Stories earlier in the book. Using a case study as well, it illustrates the way Learning Stories recognise and construct (tangled) lines of progression.

We introduce here a 'progressive filter' of a Learning Story assessment process, and we will return to this in the discussions about progress in Chapter 8. Teachers are noticing, recognising and responding to the children's learning many, many times during any one day at the early childhood, or early years, centre. Some of those occasions will be written down, recorded, as Learning Stories for portfolios.

Sharing learning experiences

Jared, this morning I was working at the mosaic table when I heard some excited chatter coming from the purple couch by the portfolios. It was you and Zavier, looking at your portfolios together.

"Look, I can do the monkey bars. I practise it", said Zavier. You looked at the Learning Story that Zavier was showing you and then started flipping through the pages in your portfolio. "I can do the monkey bars too!" you said, pointing to a story in your book.

For the next little while, you and Zavier shared your learning with each other, you showed Zavier your story about building with the train tracks, and Zavier showed you his story about making books. "I can make books too", you said.

What learning do I see happening for Jared?

Children's portfolios are a literacy artefact and play a very important part in their learning at kindergarten. We know that Jared loves his portfolio, and almost everyday he takes the opportunity to sit down and revisit his learning through this tool, sometimes on his own, and sometimes sharing his learning with his friends and teachers.

We know that children are more likely to engage in conversations about learning while using their portfolio as a tool for revisiting previous experiences. Jared used the visual pictures to help him to talk with his friend Zavier about his interests, and to learn about Zavier's interests and what they have in common.

The revisiting of prior learning experiences is one pathway in which Jared is developing his identity as a learner. It is the Learning Stories and the portfolio that enable children to recognise the learning journey that they are on. Through using his portfolio, Jared is developing the capacity for self-assessment, and for reflecting on his learning.

Jared, it was exciting to see you sharing your learning with your friend Zavier. I know how much you love your portfolio, and you took great pride in sharing the stories and photos with a friend.

Written by
Nadine

Learning Story 1.1 *Sharing learning experiences*

Author: Nadine Priebs

Many Learning Stories in a portfolio will be revisited and reviewed by the families (see Chapter 7), the teaching team and the children, as we see in Learning Story 1.1 in this chapter. In this example, the two children are reading the photographs to revisit the events in their portfolios. The teacher hears the revisiting and reviewing conversation: one of the children, Zavier, comments on a story where he is practising to climb on the monkey bars; Jared finds a parallel story, 'I can do the monkey bars too'. We note that the 'monkey bars' often appear in portfolios as a record of progress: counting the rungs achieved before the child jumps down. The teacher recognises that the portfolios 'are a literacy artefact' and they provoke conversations.

A Learning Story represents a way of assessing and teaching. The Learning Story portfolio acts as a 'boundary object' to provide two children something to talk about together, and to grow friendships: as we see in the Learning Story attached to this chapter. It is a literacy event too: in this case the children were 'reading' the photographs and talking about their common attempts to achieve success. These opportunities to 'read' a portfolio include turning the pages in sequence, and being introduced to print connected in deeply personal and emotive ways to photographs of the reader. There is research evidence that similar narrative events at home predict competence at reading (Reese et al., 2010).

The topics in Chapter 9 for **A Learning Story Workshop** mirror the chapter topics in this book. That chapter includes more questions to explore, ideas to try, topics for further thinking and collaborative activities for a team.

Learning Stories as a philosophy of assessment and learning and teaching

Learning Stories provide each teacher with the opportunity to use their authenticity, passion for life, joy and creativity to celebrate the uniqueness of each child. Learning Stories also provide the vehicle by which teachers can transform their relationships with children, parents and teachers while deepening their reflection to demonstrate teaching that makes a real difference. Carlina Rinaldi says of teaching: 'It is a difficult path that requires efforts, energies, hard work, and sometimes suffering, but it also offers wonder, amazement, joy, enthusiasm, and passion' (Rinaldi, 2006: 67). Learning Stories can: provide teachers with the opportunity to make visible the value of learning in their community, raise professionalism, develop enthusiasm for teaching and record a powerful trace of their professional life.

Although Learning Stories are a powerful tool for assessment, they are also a sociocultural philosophy of teaching. This is about the power of the learning environment and the culture of the classroom or the early childhood centre. Assessment often sits outside or alongside the teaching of the setting but assessment via Learning Stories becomes deeply embedded in the daily life of the education setting. It becomes woven into the very fabric of the teaching. It should be noted that in some Learning Stories and throughout the text of this book, we use Māori words. The meaning of these is given in a glossary at the end of the chapter where they are first mentioned.

Photo 1.1 *Storyteller Children's Center*

It is critical that children have daily access to their portfolios of Learning Stories and share them with others (children, parents and teachers) as this helps build the 'learning and teaching' culture in the setting. Vivian Gussin Paley describes how children's stories should become an embedded part of the life in the classroom. So too should Learning Stories become deeply embedded in curriculum. In sharing the stories, teachers and children are also building the learning culture of the early childhood setting. Learning Stories not only have the capacity to make learning visible, but they also strengthen relationships, build learner identities, engage the family, support transitions, evolve into planning stories and contribute to accountability. We have added a picture from the Storyteller Children's Center, Photo 1.1, designed to illustrate their philosophy about the power of stories to make learning visible. Every day, individual children's Learning Stories are selected and shared with the class.

Further thinking

- Looking back: Think of a story about learning something when you were very young.
- Why do you remember that?
- Have you noticed a young child learning something? What captured your attention?

Further reading

Carr, Margaret and Lee, Wendy (2012) *Learning Stories: Constructing Learner Identities in Early Education.* London: SAGE. Chapter 2: Why story?

New Zealand Ministry of Education (2004) *Kei tua o te Pae* Book 1 – *An Introduction to Kei Tua o te Pae*. Assessment for Learning: Early Childhood Exemplars. Downloadable at: www.education.govt.nz/assets/Documents/Early-Childhood/Kei-Tua-o-te-Pae/ECEBooklet1Full.pdf (accessed 3 December 2018).

Notes

1. In this book we use the word 'teachers' for all practitioners who care for and facilitate the learning of babies, toddlers and children outside their home. In many countries, teachers in early childhood centres are, like their primary school equivalent, 100% qualified in three-year programmes of study and practice, and we all aspire to this.

2. Wikipedia tells us the following: This is an African proverb. It means that it takes an entire community of different people interacting with children in order for a child to experience and grow in a safe environment. The villagers would look out for the children. This does not mean an entire village is responsible for raising your children and/or the children of a crowd.

2

Being Formative

Feedback which focuses on what needs to be done can encourage all to believe that they can improve. Such feedback can enhance learning, both directly through the effort that can ensue and indirectly by supporting the motivation to invest such effort. A culture of success should be promoted where every student can make achievements by building on their previous performance, rather than by being compared with others. (Assessment Reform Group, 2002: 46)

Key messages

- Assessment for learning, formative assessment, is any assessment for which the first priority in design and purpose is to promote children's learning
- Learning Stories are formative assessments
- A Learning Story assessment portfolio will include five dimensions (ABCDE)
- Learning is learnable

Teacher question: Are Learning Stories really assessments?

The quote that opens this chapter insists, from research findings, that 'feedback which focuses on what needs to be done can encourage all to believe that they can improve' and contributes to a 'culture of success' in the early childhood centre or provision. Learning Stories are narrative assessments that provide feedback to learners and their families – and to the teachers who teach them – about children's learning journeys and the strengthening, or progress, of their learning along the way. They always include the equivalent of a 'What next?' section or a suggestion within the story about what the next learning step might be, and they often refer back to earlier Learning Stories in the child's portfolio to provide evidence that the learning is progressing. In other words, the aim is to push the learning forward, and expand it, not *just* to describe an event (albeit the event might make charming reading). They are formative assessments, and evidence from research in schools indicates that we should take formative assessment seriously, because it makes a difference to learning (Black et al., 2003). In the inside cover of their booklet entitled *Working Inside the Black Box: Assessment for Learning in the Classroom*, these authors define 'Assessment *for* learning', or formative assessment, as follows (we have replaced the word 'pupils' with 'children'):

> Assessment for learning is any assessment for which the first priority in its design and practice is to serve the purpose of promoting children's learning. It thus differs from assessment designed primarily to serve the purpose of accountability, or of ranking, or of certifying competence. (Black et al., 2002, inside cover)

The word 'formative' is used in everyday English in a similar way to when we say 'that was a really formative experience', meaning that this was an experience that made a difference, had meaning for us, established or strengthened our understanding of the way forward, or caused us to recognise the significance of an earlier experience. But it is used in the assessment literature with a very specific meaning – feedback that focuses on what needs to be done to progress this learning.

Learning Stories are formative assessments

Teachers are giving verbal comments or gestures as feedback to children through-out the day. In a Learning Story, the formative suggestions are usually in a section entitled 'What next?' or 'How can we progress this learning?'; the latter acknowl-edges that this is a collaborative task that includes the teachers, the children, and sometimes the families.

When twenty booklets of Learning Stories as assessments for learning were being compiled for the Ministry of Education in Aotearoa New Zealand, we were gifted the name 'Kei tua o te pae' (New Zealand MoE, 2004a), which is a line from an *oriori* or lullaby by Hirini Melbourne. Broadly translated it means 'Beyond the horizon', and in the first booklet for that series we wrote: 'Learning is a lifelong journey that will go beyond the current horizon. The details of the journey will change as the world changes, but this vision will remain the same' (New Zealand MoE, 2004b: 5). A Learning Story will make it clear that this event belongs somewhere along a learning *journey* that is being mapped in the learner's portfolio.

An assessment portfolio will include five dimensions

An ABCD of 'being formative' was explained and explored in *Learning Stories: Constructing Learner Identities in Early Education* (for a summary see Carr and Lee, 2012: 136, and Table 2.1 below). There were originally four dimensions of learning portfolios, and in this book we add a fifth dimension.

Here are the original four dimensions, which will be further explored using examples from Learning Story portfolios.

- A stands for Agency: children initiate their own learning pathways and jour-neys and are becoming self-assessors. As their language develops, they can dialogue about their learning with increasing confidence and competence. This is the topic of Chapter 6.
- B stands for Breadth: stronger and more diverse connections are made with family and community knowledge and interests, outside the centre and the classroom. This is the topic of Chapter 7.
- C stands for Continuities: chains of learning episodes are recognised and negotiated, linking the present with the past and the future. The 'next steps' are more frequently co-constructed. So are longer term visions and possible selves. These are topics for Chapters 4 and 8.
- D stands for Distribution: the learning is distributed across an increasing number of modes of representing and communication, and they may be combined in increasingly complex ways. We call on this notion throughout the book, describ-ing a learner as a *person-plus*. This is also discussed in Chapter 6 of this book.

Table 2.1 *Purposes and consequences, balancing acts and dimensions of progress*

Purposes for and consequences of Learning Stories for children and families	AGENCY: co-authoring curriculum and assessment	BREADTH: connecting with communities outside the classroom and encouraging reciprocal engagement with families	CONTINUITIES: recognising learning journeys and the continuities of the learning over time	DISTRIBUTING: the learning across languages and modes: appropriating a repertoire of practices where the learning is distributed over a number of languages and other modes of meaning-making
Balancing goals and interests	Working things out for oneself *and* engaging in dialogue	Local classroom and early childhood centre focus *and* communicating with family and keeping the learning relevant to the wider community	Documenting expertise at one moment in time *and* constructing chains of linked episodes, finding planning directions and keeping an eye on developing learner identities	A focus on one language or mode at a time *and* a focus on an interest or open-ended task that may require a multimodal approach
Dimensions of progress	Children are initiating their own learning pathways and journeys and are becoming self-assessors	Connections are made with family and community knowledge and interests, outside the centre and the classroom	Chains of learning episodes are recognised and negotiated, linking the present with the past and the future. The 'next steps' are constructed. So are big picture visions and possible selves	The learning is distributed across a number of languages and modes of representing and communicating

Source: Carr and Lee (2012: 136), © Margaret Carr and Wendy Lee

Adding a fifth dimension: Emotion

Here we take up the challenge in the earlier book (Carr and Lee, 2012: 137–138) to add a fifth dimension: E, to suggest that formative assessments – Learning Stories and portfolios – include Emotion.

E has been added in this book. While it stands for Emotion, it also stands for enthusiasm and excitement. Sometimes teachers write of a child's 'love of literacy', or a 'love of the outdoors'. This is central to learning not only in the early years, and, indeed, across the entire lifespan. It is the major ingredient that determines whether children will engage with A, B, C and D. Teachers have always been aware of this dimension in their everyday practice, but neuroscience research has now highlighted it as a key ingredient for effective learning. Mary Helen Immordino-Yang, a neuroscientist, human development psychologist and former school teacher, summarises as follows:

> Emotions are not add-ons that are distinct from cognitive skills. Instead emotions, such as interest, anxiety, frustration, excitement, or a sense of awe in beholding beauty, become a dimension of the skill itself. This is one reason why anxiety can be so debilitating to students' performance. (Immordino-Yang, 2018: 21)

In Chapter 1 we discussed 'funds of learning disposition': being ready, willing and able to learn. The 'ready' in the 'ready, willing and able' learning disposition triad is about being motivated and interested. In the *Testing, Motivation and Learning* booklet written by the Assessment Reform Group's Assessment for Learning project, the authors comment that 'the need for "lifelong learning" places an increased emphasis on motivation. *This must come from enjoying learning and knowing how to learn*' (2002: 1; our emphasis).[1] The Assessment Reform Group's search for evidence for the role of motivation in assessment found 183 studies of which nineteen were identified as providing sound and valid empirical evidence. That booklet refers to studies in schools. However, their findings are also relevant to early childhood education contexts. In some countries testing at school entry is a common feature, and therefore testing in early childhood to prepare for the school entry tests is seen to be appropriate in some local authorities. The pressures to pass the tests push downwards. The booklet reminds us that 'when test scores are a source of pride to parents and the community, pressure is brought to bear on the school [and the contributing early childhood programmes (our addition)] for high scores' (Assessment Reform Group, 2002: 6).

Affect, emotion, is a key feature of the motivation to be ready to learn something, as the research of Mary Helen Immordino-Yang and her neuroscience colleagues has confirmed. This is further highlighted in Nel Noddings' 2003 book, *Happiness and Education*; her introduction begins as follows:

> In the past few months, when I have told people that I'm writing a book on happiness and education, more than one has responded with some puzzlement, 'But they don't go together!' … Through more than five decades of teaching and mothering, I have noticed also that children (and adults too) learn best when they are happy. (2003: 1, 2)

Handyman to the rescue: Agency, Breadth, Continuities, Distribution and Emotion

Learning Story 2.1, 'Handyman to the rescue', illustrates all these five dimensions:

A: In this example, the action (fixing a broken piece of equipment) provides Kieran with a self-assessment to do with success.

B: There is a family comment, a parent voice, sent in as a letter to be attached to the Learning Story.

C: The teacher writes, 'I remember your dad telling me stories about projects the two of you worked on'. The continuity perceived here is co-constructed with the family as 'figuring things out' and 'fixing'. Next steps (labelled here as 'Opportunities and Possibilities') describes resources that could enable Kieran not only to work on fixing, but to use his abilities and interests to create 'his own masterpieces'. A follow-on comment is added to Kieran's portfolio by Teacher Sarah:

> Kieran,
>
> Shortly after writing the 'Handyman to the rescue!' Learning Story I decided to bring out the Marble Maze and you were immediately drawn to it. I noticed you specifically looked for pieces to use to create a base and build a solid foundation. As you attached the pieces together you noticed almost immediately where the problems were. You used problem-solving skills to fix the weak link and then reconfigure the maze as needed. I observed this as I watched you create a domino run as well. You used the entire table and stood them up side by side. Initially you had the dominoes spread too far apart and some were not making contact. You addressed the issue by moving them closer to each other. Once you fixed the problem you politely invited me participate. The plan was for each of us to start at one side of the table and meet in the middle. Of course the dominoes fell down a few times before completing the domino run. It felt so good to laugh with you as we would unintentionally bump one and watch many of them fall down one on top of another.
>
> Teacher Shaun decided to start assembling the wooden launcher kit. You were one of the few children interested in helping with the project. You pulled out the directions and looked at all of materials included in the kit. It's evident that you know the importance of following directions when working on a project like this. The first few steps required gluing pieces of wood together. You gave a big squeeze on the glue bottle and the lid shot off. The two of you looked at each other with expressions of surprise and then you both let out a big burst of laughter. I love it when you laugh!
>
> Throughout the week I watched you use a variety of materials in amazing ways. This brought forth a curiosity in other classmates as they were watching you. You so generously offered assistance to friends whom you saw struggling to reproduce creations similar to yours. I mentioned in your previous Learning Story 'Flying high', that I have continually seen you kindly teach others what you know. Patiently showing them what you've learned through your own trial and error experiences. Kieran, you have a natural gift of helping others and it's so wonderful to watch.

D: Kieran is reminded of the range of resources available in the centre: 'a collection of tools' that will be made available for future projects.

E: The Learning Story writes about Kieran's 'fascination with learning how things work', indicated by the way in which he 'intently watches objects' to understand their mechanism.

HANDY "MAN" TO THE RESCUE!

Dear Kieran,

Last week when you came in to Blue Door I was feeling a little frustrated because I realised one of our scales was broken. You and your dad put me at ease when you said that you could fix it. After you washed your hands you came over to the table. With a quick look inside you said, "I think there is a loose spring inside". You picked up the Philips screwdriver and began disassembling the scale. As you were working you were focused on the task and you stated, "I know a lot of things. I've fixed like 1,000 toys". I believed this to be true since before your dad left he said you are very good at assessing a broken object and repairing it.

You carefully disassembled the scale, looked inside and said, "There is the spring". You tried to reconnect it but asked for assistance. It was indeed the spring piece that was broken just as you originally thought. We tested the scale again and again, pushing it down and pulling it up to make sure it was again in working condition.

WHAT IT MEANS?

As I watched you through the process of disassembling and reassembling you had such confidence and were quite comfortable with yourself. You were in a familiar space that I haven't seen before. I didn't have concerns about you being unsafe with the screwdriver. You demonstrated you knew how to use the tools and I could tell you had much practice. I remember your dad telling me stories about projects the two of you work on. I remember the trailer you were fixing together and the many weekends that took. It's clear you have a natural curiosity for figuring things out and using the proper tools to help fix a problem; you are a true scientist Kieran.

OPPORTUNITIES AND POSSIBILITIES

Throughout the time you have been in our class I have noticed you have a fascination with learning how things work. You always intently watch objects, such as the fidget spinners. You keenly observe them, watching to see what causes them to spin perfectly round and round. I bet if we take a look in the shed we can find some other devices to explore by deconstructing them. I will also bring out other materials such as the Crazy Forts and Marble Maze activities to help you create your own masterpieces. Blue Door has quite a collection of tools and I've been waiting for the right time to bring them out to explore with you. I look forward to many future projects together.

Teacher Sarah Macias (University California Santa Barbara, Orfalea Family Children's Center)

Learning Story 2.1 *Handyman to the rescue (part 1)*

Author: Sarah Macias

PARENT VOICE

Dear Kieran,

I loved reading Teacher Sarah's story about you helping to fix the broken scale in the Blue Door classroom. I was touched that she had noticed something about you that is so special and dear to me: your knack for fixing anything and everything. I have a memory of you, 2 years old, screwdriver in hand, helping daddy put together your new "big boy" bed. You carefully took each screw and placed it in the hold, turn by turn securing it. You turned to me and said, "I did it!" You were just a toddler but you already had the hang of the tools you would need to put things together and take them apart.

My favorite story of you fixing something is Petster. Petster, as you know, is a basketball-sized robotic kitty that was mine when I was a child around 30 years ago. It was the first robotic toy I had ever seen, and I played with him for years until eventually I got older and put him into a box filled with old toys and memories. Poor Petster languished in the box like the forgotten velveteen rabbit until last year. When we opened the box, I told you all the stories about what Petster used to do when he was still working. You were determined to make him work. You opened up his battery pack but discovered that it was corroded. We cleaned it out and eventually bought the right size batteries to put in. You switched him on but nothing happened. I shrugged my shoulders, "Oh well", I said. But you weren't willing to give up on Petster. "Let me try", you said.

That night, you spent hours tinkering with the buttons, pushing and pulling Petster around and listening to the motor and wheels whir inside of him. You noticed that the little green lights flickered on when you pushed him across the floor. You took his head in your hands and said, "Please wake up! Please wake up". But old Petster just stared blankly ahead. That night, long after you had gone to bed, I was sitting in the living room. I looked in the corner and noticed that Petster was awake, his green eyes looking at me across the room. He must have heard your wish. Petster has since become a friend to you as he was a friend when I was a kid.

I love the magical story of you fixing Petster because time and time again you have amazed me with your ability to fix objects. I love seeing the confidence you have when you are working on something, your keen sense of how pieces fit together, and your patience with these small objects. I love envisioning what you will be when you grow up – will you be a scientist? An inventor? An architect? You will be great no matter what you do. We couldn't be happier to have you as our son, and our household "Mr Fixit".

Love, Mommy

Kieran and Petster

Learning Story 2.1 *Handyman to the rescue (part 2)*
Author: Hilary Quinn

The following examples illustrate one or more of these five dimensions.

Belonging: Emotion and Breadth

Learning Story 2.2, 'Belonging', is an example that is written during Britt's early days at kindergarten. The teacher acknowledges that Britt was feeling sad when her mother left. She entitles the story 'Belonging' and also adds that 'I could tell that you were trying to be really brave in giving this kindy thing a go!'. She then adds a note to reassure 'Mum and Dad' and to begin the connection that the portfolio will make with home.

Nature girl: Agency, Distribution and Emotion (enthusiasm)

Learning Story 2.3, 'Nature girl', is an example of Ruby, who is enthusiastically initiating her own adventuring while she is in a group that takes a trip to the woods. It makes it clear that she is pursuing her interest in animals, and that this interest includes being knowledgeable: in this case 'nature smart'. In addition, the story reminds Ruby and her community at home that she was being observant and kind. A number of 'languages' and modes of representing and communication are emphasised here, including her 'reading a wilderness book at home'. So a 'tangle' of three 'languages' are highlighted here: an absent but relevant book text, Ruby's ability to read animal tracks, and her verbal explanations. We return to this notion of learning as a 'tangle' in Chapter 5 (Managing Ambiguity) and in Chapter 8 (Constructing Progress). In the latter chapter we quote Loris Malaguzzi, the first pedagogical director of the Reggio municipal schools, who describes knowledge as a 'tangle of spaghetti'; we also have more to say about language and literacy in Chapter 8.

Three stories about Noah: Agency, Breadth, Continuities, Distribution and Emotion

Learning Story 2.4 'Kia ora and welcome Noah!' is about a mobile baby Noah's first day. The teacher comments that he has 'shown a great sense of confidence to try new things'. She notes for the parents that 'the next couple of weeks are all about settling in'. The second story (2.5, 'Learning to move, moving to learn!') and third story (2.6, 'Mana whenua: developing a sense of belonging') highlight the continuity of his settling: interacting with other very young children, playing with a series of sound-makers, and making the most of opportunities to explore at just the right level. The stories track his increasing ability to move around, and his enjoyment of the resources as modes for making sounds and sensorial explorations. Two of the three stories include a 'conversation' between the family and the teacher.

The feeling of belonging, in the widest sense, contributes to one's inner well-being, security and identity.

Our Early Childhood Curriculum Te Whāriki conveys the importance of providing an environment where children and their families know they have a place. Where a feeling of belonging and having a right to belong in an early childhood setting is central to the philosophy and actions of those in the environment.

Britt, I know that you were feeling sad when your Mum left kindergarten today. After a passage of time and when you were ready to have a cuddle you decided that you just wanted to hang out with me. Together we had morning tea, read some books and you even helped me do some jobs.
I could tell that you were trying to be really brave in giving this kindy thing a go!
As the day wore on your confidence grew and an independent spirit came to light. You confidently chatted to a number of children and involved yourself in their games and play.

Mum and Dad we really want to support Britt's kindergarten journey and we know that she will have heaps of fun here with us.
We also know it is important for children to develop relationships that encompass a sense of trust and belonging when they start in a new early childhood setting.

Developing a relationship with Britt so that elements of belonging and well being can be explored are our initial focus.

We hope that Britt's portfolio will support the sharing of 'funds of knowledge' about the things that she enjoys doing at home and the things that she is learning about here at kindergarten. That it will be a tool to support this notion of trust and belonging to evolve.
Welcome to Albany Kindergarten Britt, we are so excited to have you and your family as part of our learning community.

written by Kaiako Fran

Learning Story 2.2 *Belonging*
Author: Fran Paniora

Nature Girl

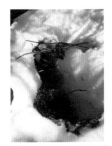

Today Ruby you were such an adventurer. You were so excited when you found an animal home first thing when we got to the woods. You told me, 'Come and look, I found a hedgehog's home'.

Then you, Rose, Gabby and Lane were off to follow animal tracks. You told us all that you were good at finding animal tracks because you were reading a wilderness book at home. You found some horse tracks and told us what eagle tracks looked like, explaining that their toes are all spread out so that they could pick up their food. You are so nature smart!

You said yes you were and that you were a real nature girl. You trudged on through the deep snow and called out to us to "come on". You were so kind and helpful as you held back the branches for us so we could come through the gnarly trees. I had so much fun on our adventure today! When I am in the woods I like to stick with you because you know so much about the animals in the forest.

"Look deep into nature and then you will understand everything better."

Albert Einstein

What did I learn about Ruby today, and what opportunities are ahead?
Maybe next time we go out in the forest we could bring along some pictures of footprints to help us identify animal prints. I wonder if Ruby would like to share her wilderness book with us, it sounds so interesting. As you play you are developing a sense of wonder and appreciation for the natural world, connecting and showing respect for nature and taking pleasure in natural beauty. You are also learning to employ creative approaches to identify and work out practical problems as you raise questions and make hypotheses about how and why things happen, such as foot prints. You are learning to observe, name and record and investigate natural phenomena. This helps you to recognize and record patterns and relationships in nature encouraging a future as an environmental steward, ensuring sustainable futures.

Written by
Kendra

Learning Story 2.3 *Nature girl*
Author: Kendra Womacks

Kia ora and welcome Noah!

KIA ORA AND WELCOME NOAH!

Today we welcomed a new friend to Bear Park, Noah!

Noah, you had such an amazing first day! You spent lots of time getting to know your new teachers and friends as well as your new environment. You really enjoyed the music space, reading books and investigating all the mirrors and reflective materials. You were very curious as you explored the many resources on offer and you were also quite entranced watching your older friends.

Noah, the next couple of weeks are all about settling in and developing a sense of belonging here at Bear Park. We really look forward to getting to know you and your family more and sharing your learning journey with them!

Parent comment: Noah had a great day and will sleep well tonight. Thank you for the wonderful welcome.

Learning Story 2.4 *Kia ora and welcome Noah!*

Author: Hiromi McCarthy-Dowd

Learning to move, moving to learn!

Noah, you have continued to settle in well and have clearly found your place in the Fantail room. A very clear sign of this is the way you have shown us your confidence to master the challenge of trying to move. This has definitely been your focus for the last month. It has been an amazing process to observe and support you with.

You started with rolling onto your tummy and then turning round and round, following everything that catches your interest. From here you explored other ways of moving your body. I noticed you experimenting with your toes, digging them in as if trying to push off. You were also using your arms, stretching right out to objects that were just out of your reach. Soon I noticed that you were in fact shuffling your body forward while exploring but you didn't seem to notice, as you were fully engaged in exploring the many things that captured your interest. You were also pushing up with your arms into a press up style position you amazed us all with your strength!

Noah, as soon as you had mastered how to move your body forward, you have been finding new ways to challenge yourself physically. You are confidently sitting yourself up and move from sitting to crawling and back again with ease. You are also using furniture to pull yourself up onto your feet and have even tried to let go with one hand - your confidence and body awareness is amazing! You have such a look of delight as you make all these new discoveries, showing just how much you are enjoying your journey of learning how to move.

Teacher reflection

In the Fantail room a strong part of our philosophy is giving children the time and space to learn to move naturally. Through providing this time and space, the children have the opportunity to truly discover their bodies. They are developing spatial and body awareness, self-confidence, balance, coordination and strength. Through this they are also developing a positive self-image of themselves as capable, they believe in themselves and are confident to give new things a go.

"Whilst learning to move, children are not only learning about their bodies and its movements, but also how to learn. They are learning how to do something on their own, to be interested, to try out, to experiment. They learn to overcome difficulties. They come to know the joy and the satisfaction which is derived from this success. The result of patience and persistence." (Parentingworx, 2009)

Noah, through your journey of learning to move you have set yourself challenges and worked to overcome these, developing your problem solving skills and ability to persevere. These are skills and dispositions you will continue to develop and draw on in all aspects of your learning. You have also shown how adventurous you are - as soon as you have mastered one challenge you are setting yourself another challenge!

I look forward to seeing where you go next Noah, what will capture your interest now you are on the move? Will you continue to focus on physical challenges? Or perhaps you will discover something new?

Family Voice

Erin and Neil, what has Noah been interested in exploring at home now that he is on the move?
Thanks Hiromi, this is so special to see!

Noah loves exploring at home too. The kitchen seems to be his favourite place at the moment and he can reach the handles for the drawers which he uses to stand up. He has also started opening the cupboard doors to see what is inside. He loves going to the windows to see our dog, Molly. This always makes him smile.

Teacher's voice

Thanks Erin, it's great to hear how Noah is exploring similar interests at home. With his curious nature I can just imagine how much fun he is having discovering what's in your kitchen.

Learning Story 2.5 *Learning to move, moving to learn!*

Author: Hiromi McCarthy-Dowd

Mana Whenua – developing a sense of belonging

Noah, it's hard to believe it's nearly been a month since you started here at Bear Park. You have settled in with such ease! You are clearly happy to be here, smiling, chatting and kicking your legs to show us your excitement. During your transition visits we were able to establish a strong trusting relationship before your first day. I was able to spend lots of time with you, finding out about all your likes, dislikes, interests, strengths and getting to know you. I'm very excited to be your special buddy and think we've already developed a great relationship. This is made very clear through the way you greet me with a massive grin every morning as well as reaching out to me to ask for cuddles throughout the day.

I have noticed that you have a very curious nature, you want to be on the floor exploring, reaching out for everything that catches your interest. You are becoming more and more mobile and I think this is in part driven by your curiosity.

You are very observant and enjoy sitting and watching your friends. You have shown an interest in lots of different parts of our classroom such as the construction space; exploring mirrors and reflection; the music space and also looking at books. You are always so engaged as you focus and concentrate on what has caught your interest.

You have also shown a great sense of confidence to try new things. You are a very sensory explorer and have investigated many different textures such as the clay and sand. These were new experiences for you at Bear Park, however you confidently got involved, digging your fingers in and scratching through both of the clay and sand. I wonder if you have explored similar things at home?

Teacher reflection

Noah, this month has been all about settling in and finding your place through getting to know your new learning environment, your teachers and your friends. You have amazed us all with how well you have already settled into Bear Park life. I think the slow transition process where we slowly spent time getting to know each other has worked well. You have quickly gained confidence and are clearly developing a strong sense of belonging.

Our early childhood curriculum, Te Whāriki, highlights the importance of this through stating that "Children and their families feel a sense of belonging" and "...know that they have a place" (p.54) and I believe this is true for you Noah.

I will continue to support you with developing this sense of belonging Noah and look forward to sharing many exciting learning moments with you and your family throughout your time in the Fantail room.

Family voice

Erin and Neil, how have you found the transition process? We would love to hear your ideas and thoughts about how Noah is settling in.

Thank you Hiromi for you feedback on Noah, we are so pleased that he has settled in well. He seems so happy to get to Bear Park and sleeps well after a day of adventures in the Fantail Room. I think his learning has accelerated with watching his friends crawl and move around the room. I hope he remains settled as we increase his days and hours at Bear Park in the next few weeks. Our home life will change a bit as I return to work but I feel very comfortable that Noah will be happy with you and his friends at Bear Park.

Teacher's voice

Hi Erin, Noah has adjusted well to his longer days and has continued to be his happy, curious and adventurous self! He is very settled and confidently explores everything on offer. The way you organised such a slow transition has definitely paid off!

Learning Story 2.6 *Mana whenua – developing a sense of belonging*
Author: Hiromi McCarthy-Dowd

Butterfly getting eaten

Distribution, Agency, Emotion and a 'passion' for butterflies

In Learning Story 2.7, 'Butterfly getting eaten!' (see next page), Jamie writes a story (see below). This combines drawing and dictating a four-part sequential story illustrated by a series of drawings. The teacher writes to Jamie and includes the question, 'What learning is happening here?', emphasising the sequence of events (each page includes 'Then … or Next …'), the good and bad characters, and her 'passion for butterflies'. She also notes that 'this story drew on your interest for and knowledge of butterflies and crabs, and your own life experiences such as going to the beach, taking a nature walk, and attending a party'. This gives this Learning Story a place, in time, in her portfolio and thus emphasises the formative, ongoing, aspect of Learning Stories.

Butterfly getting eaten!

Written and illustrated by Jamie

Page 1: One day there was caterpillars and then turned into chrysalis and then into butterflies. And then they turned back into a chrysalis and caterpillar again. Caterpillars are going to eat swan plants and turn back into a chrysalis and butterfly again.

Page 2: The butterflies are going to have a nature walk and they are going to find friend butterflies they are going to meet.

Then they are going to go to the beach to have a swim and find a crab.

Page 3: Then they are going to go for a swim in the deepest water and find fish. They are going to go back to their island and go home and have a sleep and then wake up and have lunch. Next they have breakfast and dinner.

Page 4: A monster took one butterfly away and ate it and there was ten thousand butterflies left and they killed the monster. Then they had a party and they had some candy and some lollies at the party and M and Ms and they lived happily every after.

Author: Jamie Kirchhain

Butterfly getting eaten!
by April Jensen

Jamie, a while ago I asked you if you could come and tell me a story; at first you told me that you didn't know any stories but then I explained that I wanted you to make one up. I said it could be about anything you like. You started to tell me a story about butterflies; I wrote the whole thing down. It was such a great story that I decided to turn it into a book, so I wrote it out over four pages, then asked you to come and illustrate it. I read out each page for you and you drew a picture to represent the story. When you had done all four pages I asked you what you would like to call your story and you came up with "Butterfly getting eaten". I wrote that down and then you drew a picture to go with it for your cover page. Later on I laminated each page and bound them together, and now you have your very own book – written and illustrated by you!

What learning is happening here?
Jamie, you have a very creative imagination along with a passion for butterflies (among other things) and coming up with your own story was a great outlet for this. In making this book you have started learning the process for book construction – you tell the story, it gets written down, you draw the pictures to go with it, you make a cover page, and we bind it. You are also developing the skill of creating an original story; to do this you created a beginning, a series of events, and an ending complete with good and bad characters. Your story drew on your interest for and knowledge of butterflies and crabs, and your own life experiences such as going to the beach, taking a nature walk, and attending a party.

What was remarkable about this experience for you is how the book construction activity provided not only its own learning opportunity but an opportunity for you to bring together your knowledge of how stories are told with your passions, interests and life experiences. I can't wait to read this book at mat time to show your peers just how special this book of yours is!

Learning Story 2.7 *Butterfly getting eaten!*

Author: April Jeusen

Dennis's wonderful jump: Agency, Emotion and the joy of mastering a challenge

In Learning Story 2.8, 'Dennis's wonderful jump', Dennis has found something of interest to him, and he has been invited by the teacher to accomplish a challenge. His persistence is noted, and the teacher reminds him and his family, who will read this Learning Story, that 'This week it was mastering the jump challenge, in the future it might be struggling with a maths problem or tackling a tricky reading challenge; it is all the same principle, be courageous, give things a go and try, and your efforts are bound to be rewarded with success!'.

Huddy hammering: Agency, Distribution, Emotion, a deep concentration on a self-chosen task

Learning Story 2.9, 'Huddy hammering', is about a developing project, initiated by the child, to 'make the wood silver', to cover a space. Hammering needs focus, concentration and eye–hand coordination. The teacher introduces counting for a purpose: she assists him to count the 38 nails that in the end (after this photograph was taken) contributed to his ambition.

Learning is learnable

Guy Claxton has said that 'Learning is Learnable, (And We Ought To Teach It)' (Claxton, 2004: 237). These assessments remind the learners and the families of that. Furthermore, Guy Claxton and colleagues have this to say in their book *The Learning Powered School* (Claxton et al., 2011: 3):

> We think that our society's notion of 'ability' has been too closely tied to academic achievement, and to the assumption that some youngsters have got a lot of that sort of ability and some not very much. We think that real-world intelligence is broader than that, and that it is not fixed at birth, but something that can be helped to build up.

Learning Stories are formative assessments. They are part of the *teaching process*. They work in the same way as a comment from, or a collaboration with, the teacher, but these comments last much longer. As we noted in Chapter 1, the written 'comment' or the memory of the event is reified (made 'concrete', permanent, able to be read by others, including the children who can read) because the learner, other children, other teachers and family members can return to it. The 'What next?' for the learning is recorded so that, unlike a comment, a fleeting smile, or thumbs up it can be revisited again and again. Although it may be recorded at the end of the day it occurs, or later, it nevertheless is not lost amongst memories about learning during the hurly burly of a busy centre or school day.

For the older children, the stories encourage *self-assessment* by the children: sharing goals with them, and helping them to notice and recognise that what they are doing is an example or an opportunity that connects with the framing in the

Dennis's Wonderful Jump!

你好

Nǐ hǎo

Dear Dennis,
I put the plank up high and children started to walk along it and jump off. This is sort of an extension of the spring board challenge I set up the other day. I asked you if you would like a turn. You shook your head and looked at me as though you thought I might just be a wee bit crazy! "Maybe you might like to try later", I suggested. You walked away to play somewhere else. Then a little while later you came back, your curiosity was getting the better of you I think. You stood watching for a while. "I could hold your hand", I said. You agreed and so it was, you climbed up on to the plank and I held your hand and then you jumped, wheee! You asked me to hold your hand one more time and then you didn't need me to any more. Oh boy Dennis, you quickly mastered this plank walking and jumping challenge and soon you were not only WALKING across the plank, you were RUNNING!!! And you didn't just JUMP off, you FLEW OFF, launching yourself into the air so high that when you landed you had reached the very end of the mat!!!! WOW WOW WOW!!!!!

My thoughts on your learning
Moments like these are what I live for, Dennis! To see you develop your confidence from not wanting to try, to becoming involved with support, to launching yourself like a supernova!!! This is the joy of being a teacher, to be able to support you and other children to grow and realise your amazing potential!

Where to next?
When you next face something that you are not sure of, remember how when you give things a go, and do some practice, you can fly! Life is full of so many exciting learning adventures!

This week it was mastering the jump challenge, in the future it might be struggling with a maths problem or tackling a tricky reading challenge, it is all the same principle, be courageous, give things a go and try, and your efforts are bound to be rewarded with success!

Thank you Dennis! Love Julie

Learning Story 2.8 *Dennis's wonderful jump*
Author: Julie Killick

Huddy Hammering

Oh my goodness Huddy! You really are quite AMAZING!!! Today I saw you banging in lots of nails into one piece of wood. You told me you wanted to make the wood silver. We counted up your nails, in English and in te reo. I was so impressed with your counting AND your incredible hammering skills! When you had finished you had hammered in a total of 38 nails! Those nails just FLEW into the wood under your expert hammering, straight and true! WOW!!!

You know to get this good at hammering you must have done A LOT of practising! See! Practice pays off – I can imagine you whacking in big nails making a shed, or a deck or a house when you are a big man! Ka pai mahi!

What learning is happening here?
Huddy, I just love your passion and gusto! You threw yourself into this hammering project of yours 150% No holding back! This approach is very powerful! Your determination and commitment to the task meant that you achieved your goal, and today the goal you set yourself was to make a silver coating on the wood, tomorrow or sometime off in the future your goals may be very different, but one thing is for sure – if you approach them with the same attitude you will be crowned with success – what could stand in the way of such energy and enthusiasm!?! I LOVE IT! Also today you practised your skills in counting and te reo!

How can we support your learning further?
Huddy, you know we are here to support you in all the goals you set yourself. We will also make sure we keep the wood and nail supply well stocked up!

Love Julie

Learning Story 2.9 *Huddy hammering*
Author: Julie Killick

curriculum, and the values espoused there (and here, at the centre or school). The self-assessment is linked to both the child and the task and to valuable learning aims and principles, not to a more global judgement of a 'disconnected' person.

An assessment provides feedback for families that illustrates next steps in the learning and how they can take them with confidence in other contexts. Revisiting the stories with children at the centre and the home is a reminder of features of a learner identity that will serve them well in the future. Reviewing portfolios within the teaching team enables teachers to share their written Learning Stories, to discuss stories they are about to write and to seek advice from each other about a 'What next?' commentary. This depends on the teaching staff having time to do this. Wendy has worked closely on professional learning with teachers and we recognise the many calls on teachers' time at work away from children or students. Enlightened governments and educational funding providers will provide for time for teachers to write stories, discuss them with other teachers and talk to families. We see this staff time as critical to the growth of strong assessment practice and we refer to this time as 'teachers researching their practice'.

The writing of a Learning Story can be formative for the teachers too. At the end of a group Learning Story about a science project in which the children collected Monarch butterflies and caterpillars and chrysalises, one of the teachers, Helen, wrote, commenting that 'fifty-two butterflies had been raised and released by the children':

> We, as teachers, have learned through this project how important it is to record every step of the learning process, not just the products, as this (recording) tells us about the depth of learning that goes on. One of the other most significant things to us was the number of children involved here. There was a real sense of belonging evident. All of us learned together, teachers included. There were several times when Dawn and I said: 'I don't know. How could we find out?' (New Zealand MoE, 2004c: 20)

A Learning Story often highlights *the surrounding circumstances* that made this learning possible and/or enjoyable. This is a very significant point, and we consider it in the next chapter, Being Fair.

Further thinking

1. A formative assessment suggests a way forward for the learner, and this chapter has illustrated five dimensions of an assessment that would make a 'What next?'. Which of these features do you want to think about further?
2. Think back on a conversation with a friend. What kinds of comments or contributions did you add that kept the conversation going?

3. Think about the contexts (teaching, or in everyday life outside teaching) when, like Helen and Dawn at the end of this chapter, you have said something like: 'I don't know. How could we find out?' What happened next?
4. Think about a context that is relevant to your own learning progress. Which dimensions are relevant for your current 'What next?' and how are they combined in your context?

Further reading

Black, Paul and Wiliam, Dylan (2006) Developing a theory of formative assessment. In J. Gardner (ed.), *Assessment and Learning*. London: SAGE, pp. 81–100.

Carr, Margaret and Lee, Wendy (2012) *Learning Stories: Constructing Learner Identities in Early Education*. London: SAGE. Chapter 1: Learner identities in early education: Introduction to four themes.

Note

1. The members of the Assessment Reform Group: Professor Paul Black, Professor Patricia Broadfoot, Professor Richard Dougherty, Professor Wynn Harlen, Dr Mary James. Dr Gordon Stobart, Professor Dylan Wiliam.

Kaiako = Teacher(s)
Kia ora = Hello, be well
Mana = The power of being, authority, prestige, spiritual power, integrity, status and control
Te reo = Māori language

3

Being Fair

We will listen to Jason's helicopter stories and offer our own in exchange. In this evolving classroom drama every revelation is necessary and equally important, for our goal is more than fantasy. It is fairness. (Vivian Gussin Paley, 1990: xii)

Although rethinking assessment has remained one important goal of our work, our interest in assessment has come to be framed in terms of the intersection between assessment and OTL [opportunity to learn]. (Pamela Moss, Diana Pullin, James Paul Gee, Edward Haertel and Lauren Jones Young, 2008: 5)

Key messages

- Learning environments can be not fair
- A learning disposition is about being ready, willing and able to learn: *being willing* is about the learning environment and the OTL
- Learning Stories will recognise the person-plus

Teacher question: Is there a key feature of Learning Stories assessments that tests can't do?

Learning environments can be not fair

Two adults' stories

We open this chapter with two stories: one from a teacher and writer (Vivian Gussin Paley), and the second from a psychologist and writer (Carol Dweck). They tell stories about themselves which illustrate facilitating environments that were *not fair*. They both write about a shift in the *opportunity to learn*.

Story one: Carol Dweck, a psychologist, writes vividly about the role of motivation in teaching and learning in relation to someone making an assessment of her ability. She tells a story from her own schooling (2006: 74, 75).

> I was once a math whiz. In high school, I got 99 in Algebra, a 99 in geometry, and a 99 in trigonometry, and I was on the math team. I scored up there with the boys on the air force test of visual-spatial ability, which is why I got recruiting brochures from the air force for many years to come. Then I got a Mr Hellman, a teacher who didn't believe girls could do math. My grades declined, and I never took math again.

Dweck refers here to a change in the teacher that created a change in the culture of the classroom. The culture of the early childhood centre or school classroom ought to encourage (give courage to) all children to believe that intelligence can expand and success can be gained: learning goals. Of course, every teacher has on many occasions established *performance goals* (the rules of appropriate behaviour in this space). Dweck, however, reminds us of a higher ambition – that the *teachers* will constantly work towards a culture, a climate, where *learning goals* are highlighted in their early childhood centre or classroom setting.

Story two: Vivian Paley tells a similar personal story to Carol Dweck's in her book *Bad Guys Don't Have Birthdays: Fantasy Play at Four* (1988: 6, 7). When she was aged twenty, she led a Great Books discussion in the New Orleans Public Library, and she arrived each day with a list of printed questions that she intended to follow. She implies that the participants took no notice of her list of questions when she writes that 'The participants were older and wiser, but my lists of questions made me brave'. She now re-defines the distractions from a planned curriculum guide as 'the sounds of the children thinking' (for themselves):

> Soon after, I became a kindergarten teacher and had curriculum guides instead of printed questions. I still believed it was my job to fill the time quickly with a minimum of distractions, and the appearance of a correct answer gave me the surest feeling that I was teaching. It did not occur to me that the distractions might be the sounds of the children thinking. (Paley, 1988: 6–7)

In education, in early years provision or school, the learning environment should encourage all children to believe that success can be gained. It should facilitate the courage to *be willing* to engage in some difficult tasks, tasks that they are not sure they can easily accomplish. This sociocultural perspective – the relationship between learning and a learning environment – is classically known as the 'opportunity to learn' (OTL). In the book *Assessment, Equity, and Opportunity to Learn* (Moss et al., 2008), the authors write the following in the Introduction:

> Our socioculturally informed learning theory reminds us that assessment practices are inevitably elements of learning environments that shape (enable and constrain) learning and opportunities to learn. (2008: 10)

The two personal stories that began this chapter (Vivian Gussin Paley's and Carol Dweck's) provided examples from their earlier lives in which they interpreted a learning (Dweck) or teaching (Paley) environment as one that did not enable two vital elements of OTL environments: belonging (to the community of successful maths students: Dweck), and being collaborative (teaching that included sharing the responsibility with others: Paley). These were examples of situations in which Carol Dweck did not feel that she belonged in the mathematics class, and Vivian Paley did not feel that she ought to listen to contributions from the people she was teaching. Both of them subsequently changed their mindsets, and the educational world has greatly benefited from their wisdom because of it.

A learning disposition is about being ready, willing and able to learn: *being willing* is about interpreting the learning environment

Guy Claxton (1990: 164) has commented that 'it can be strongly argued that schools' major responsibility must be to help young people become ready, willing and able to cope with change successfully: that is, to be powerful and effective learners'. David Perkins, Eileen Jay and Shari Tishman (1993: 1) introduced three components of a 'thinking disposition' to the literature on learning as inclination, sensitivity to occasion, and ability. The 2001 Learning Story book, *Assessment in Early Childhood Settings* (Carr, 2001), described learning dispositions as 'situated learning strategies plus motivation', and as being 'ready, willing and able' to learn:

> If we take the example of communication, or expressing one's ideas, then *being ready* is being motivated or inclined to communicate, *being willing* is recognising that the situation is an appropriate one in which to express one's ideas, and *being able* is the communication skills and understandings that will be needed for this occasion. (Carr, 2001: 9)

Chapter 2 in this book was about *being ready*: the emotions that motivate children to want to participate and engage. Perhaps the more unfamiliar of these features is *being willing* or *sensitive to occasion*. Children may take some time to 'suss out' what is deemed to be acceptable in a new environment that is not at all like home. Teachers too. When the authors of this book were student teachers on 'practicum' and newly appointed teachers, we became very sensitive to, and aware of, the culture of different early childhood environments. Before we had a national curriculum, centres came with a range of expectations. These provided indications about what was admirable, and what was not, and children and new teachers had to work out the relationships and the acceptable behaviour. This culture is sometimes called the 'hidden curriculum', and many children become very competent at reading the culture of the classroom or the early childhood centre. But some children do not. At its best, the environment encourages a viewpoint that it is OK to try something difficult and risk failing, knowing that trying again is possible and viewed with enthusiasm by the teachers. At its worst it can discourage experimentation and encourage compliance, limiting the opportunity to learn, and disrupting any assessment practice that includes a positive view of curiosity or creativity. These are children's interpretations of the classroom's or early childhood centre's social environment. The two – being ready and being willing – both have emotional content. Mary Helen Immordino-Yang, the neuroscientist introduced in Chapter 2, made the comment that:

> for school-based learning to have a hope of motivating students, of producing deep understanding, or of transferring into real-world skills – all hallmarks of meaningful learning, and all essential to producing informed, skilled, ethical and reflective adults – we need to find ways to leverage the emotional aspects of learning in education. ... When I say that many emotions are 'complex', what I really mean is that they rely on subjective, cognitive *interpretations of situations* and their accompanying embodied reactions. (Immordino-Yang, 2018: 18–19; our emphasis)

This aspect of a learning disposition, being sensitive to, and able to interpret an occasion, insists that even if a child is ready and able to take some action in one context, any other context must feel safe, open, interesting and engaging enough to enable, permit – and (probably) encourage and welcome – that action. We provide examples of two categories of 'being willing'. One is interpreting the *situation*: 'Is it interesting?' 'Is it safe?' 'Do I have a place here?'. The second emphasises the *surround*: 'What supports me here?'

Literacy in the bush: interpreting the situation

Learning Story 3.1, 'Literacy in the bush', is an example of a group of children from an early childhood centre visiting, regularly, local nature reserves. The teacher writes an introduction:

> On our farm adventures we often walk public tracks. The children love to spot markers along the way. We know that orange markers show us where the track leads and pink markers show us where the trapping lines run. Charlie, however, noticed something else today. 'Look, look, there's a two and a zero', he called to us.

The teacher notes that 'we often stop to decode signs on these adventures'. This might be described as reading environmental codes and signs – for a purpose. In one of the photographs, the teacher and the children are reading the symbols on a sign: the symbol (a picture of a kiwi bird) indicates that kiwi birds' habitations are near here. This is a motivating environment for introducing signs – letters, numbers and pictures – as useful literacy objects.

Puff the Magic Dragon: interpreting the surround, the resources on offer

Sometimes it is said that children can get 'hooked on reading', and this includes relishing those occasions when reading a book is exciting and emotionally engaging. Learning Story 3.2, 'Puff the Magic Dragon', is an example. It combines a sad song and a sad story, and in this case the listener to the story is in a safe and comforting environment: on the teacher's lap with a familiar book. This is not the first time that Ayzah has had this experience of singing and turning the pages together with the teacher. Her English language is enough for her to express her emotion: 'Ohh, he sad', 'Where his friend?', 'Ohh, he gone'.

Environments change people

In Learning Story 3.3, 'Environments change people', from Japan, the parent makes a wise comment about 'being willing' to learn: 'I realise that environments change people'. Her daughter would not touch insects at home, but at the early childhood provision she was encouraged and supported to be willing to touch the bugs. The parent adds another quality to this event, adding a powerful framing, *kindness*, to her analysis of this experience. We will write more about these wider narratives in Chapter 4.

Learning Stories will recognise the person-plus

If an assessment is to be fair, it must take account of the features of the world that possibly or probably enhance or diminish the opportunity to learn. David Perkins

Literacy in the bush

On our farm adventures we often walk public tracks the children love to spot markers along the way. We know now that orange markers show us where the track leads and pink markers show us where the trapping lines run. Charlie however, noticed something else today.

"Look, look, there's a 2 and a 0",

he called to us all.

Unpacking the learning for Charlie

Our forest farm adventures are rich in so very many ways. These are the moments that remind us that our adventures into the wild are full of opportunities to identify and decode symbols and text, but in ways that are meaningful and contextual for the children. It gave us the opportunity to have a discussion about the purpose of numbering trapping lines and appreciate the need for numbers in our lives. It is with this knowledge that children then have purpose and meaning for their continued learning, whatever it might be.

Where might this learning lead?

We often stop to decode signs on these adventures and I know that there will be many more opportunities to explore literacy. I wonder what Charlie will notice next and how he might share his knowledge about numbers and letters with his friends. I will certainly encourage him to be leaderful in this area and I will support and value Charlie's learning whatever it might be.

Arohanui, Melissa

Learning Story 3.1 *Literacy in the bush*

Author: Melissa Osmond

Puff the Magic Dragon

A sad and touching song

> *"Puff the magic dragon lives by the sea"*

These photos capture one of our many recent readings/singing of *Puff the Magic Dragon* together Ayzah. We seem to share a love and attachment to this beautiful song, and book. It is pretty special isn't it?

The lyrics of the song (originally a poem written in 1959) tell a story of the dragon named Puff and his playmate, Jackie Paper, a little boy. Jackie Paper eventually grows up, and loses interest in the imaginary adventures of childhood and then leaves Puff. Although the song ends in this way, the illustrated book shows a girl on the last page – maybe a new companion and friend for Puff?

The other day when we first sang and turned the pages together you showed such genuine and heartfelt compassion for the characters and themes within the song/story, Ayzah. You may not have all of the English words yet (or even words in your first language Urdu) to explain your thinking, but your responses, attention and body language cut straight to the heart and meaning of the tale and I believe that you are understanding these on a deep level.
"Ohh, he sad", you said, pointing to Puff, when Jackie Paper comes no more.
"Where his friend?" you asked me (of Jackie Paper). *"Ohh, he gone"*.
Feelings of loneliness or sadness are universal and you were able to understand and relate to this. I have heard you sing some of the lyrics in the last few days and yesterday and today you asked me to read this together again. Thank you for sharing this beautiful story with me Ayzah.
Helen

Learning Story 3.2 *Puff the Magic Dragon*
Author: Helen Aitken

Environments Change

Yuna build a special house for the pill bugs. The pill bugs walked into the house and they looked so happy. You said 'Welcome to the pill house'. I think your kindness is beautiful! Your kindness is a treasure.

Yuna's mother's comments:

My daughter does not like bugs and I also do not like bugs. I was surprised to see the photo because, before, my daughter would not touch insects.

I realise that environments change people. Yuna has been encouraged and supported to touch the bugs. Also, I realise that she can take care of animals and young children. I hope you will grow to be a gentle daughter.

Learning Story 3.3 *Environments change*

Author: Saki Inanobe

(2009b: 88–110) described the learner as a 'person-plus' in a chapter on the implications of this for teaching and learning. He reminds us that, when we consider thinking and learning, we should take as our unit of analysis not the learner without resources, but the *person plus* the surround. Perkins makes the point that 'the surround – the immediate physical and social resources outside the person – participates in cognition, not just as a source of input, but as a vehicle of thought' (2009b: 90). He gives the label of 'person-solo' to the notion of a person on their own without the social and material resources for learning. He adds (and we have added 'website') in a nice turn of phrase:

> Schools mount a consistent campaign to make the person-plus a 'person-solo'. 'Person plus pencil, paper, text, almanac, encyclopaedia [and website]' and so on is fine for *studying*, but the target performance is typically 'person plus paper and pencil'. And the pencil and paper are conceived not so much as thinking aids as a hopper into which the person-solo can pour concrete evidence of achievement.[1] (Perkins, 2009b: 95)

In other words, it is not just in early childhood that children depend on material resources to support their everyday learning; we all learn this way. For the writers of this book, the *person-plus* includes the books on our shelves and libraries, our notebooks, our computers, websites and the many, many, thoughtful writers who have gone before and encouraged us to persevere. Being willing is not fair if this situation, while it looks safe, diminishes the supportive tools and resources – and companions – that learners, and writers, need.

It's tricky!

Learning Story 3.4, 'It's tricky!', is an example of 'being willing' in both senses: the 'situation' and the 'surround'. The Learning Story notes that Zibin has already been responding to challenging problems, and this is a further example. In both challenges the situation included other children in support. In the first case, another child assisted with a difficult bridging problem and a water flow in the environment provided the stimulus for the task he had set himself, to enable the toy cars to cross a bridge over the water. The second challenge, finding pairs, needed the game pieces and it also attracted an audience to admire his ability and perhaps to assist.

One-to-one correspondence

Learning Story 3.5, 'One-to-one correspondence', began from Blake's interest in numbers: noticed, recognised and responded to here. The teacher recognised that, because of this interest, he would probably be ready and willing to be engaged in an extended number task: to connect the written numbers up to ten with the appropriate number of objects, to sequence the size of the groups, and to write the number symbols. The resources are available for this. The Learning Story indicates that Blake had already shown an interest in solving problems using numbers. Adding to his identity as a person-plus, he was photographing

"It's tricky!"

Written by Jessica

Zibin, I've been noticing how you respond to challenges in your learning at kindergarten this week. First I watched you in the creek with your friend Drew as you both worked together to build a bridge across the water flow for your trains. But it wasn't turning out the way you had hoped – the tracks were unbalanced and they kept falling and breaking apart! I watched you take a pause and think … before sharing your idea with Drew and skipping off to find what you needed to solve the problem. The next day, you joined in on a memory game with your friends. **"It's tricky!"** you exclaimed as you tried to find a match, waited patiently for your turn, and tried again. You never gave up though Zibin and just look at the photo of your big smile when you finally found two bears that were the same! You were so happy with your achievement after all of that time waiting, noticing the bears when your friends had a turn, thinking about which bears matched and remembering where they were located – a very big challenge!

What did I learn about Zibin today?

Learning can be tricky Zibin, but these photos capture how deeply involved you are in many spaces both indoors and outdoors. Your enthusiasm for learning is contagious and it is a joy to be learning with you as you confidently share your ideas with us and continue to think and explore possibilities as you tackle the challenge. What a strong learner you are Zibin – a kindy friend that we can all learn from as we stretch and grow ourselves this year at kindergarten.

What next

We will continue to note the different spaces and places in which you attempt to stay with difficult tasks.

> "The passion for stretching yourself and sticking to it, even when it's not going well, is the hallmark of the growth mindset. This is the mindset that allows people to thrive during the most challenging times of their life." Carol Dweck

Learning Story 3.4 *It's tricky!*

Author: Jessica Dubois

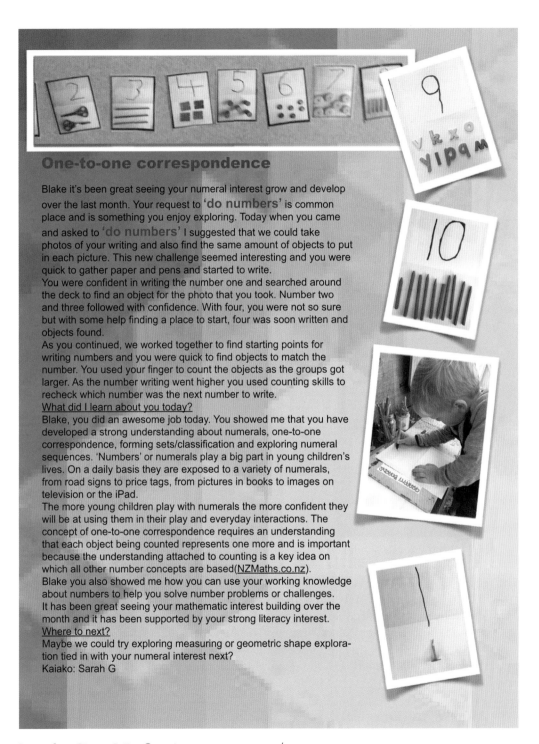

One-to-one correspondence

Blake it's been great seeing your numeral interest grow and develop over the last month. Your request to 'do numbers' is common place and is something you enjoy exploring. Today when you came and asked to 'do numbers' I suggested that we could take photos of your writing and also find the same amount of objects to put in each picture. This new challenge seemed interesting and you were quick to gather paper and pens and started to write.

You were confident in writing the number one and searched around the deck to find an object for the photo that you took. Number two and three followed with confidence. With four, you were not so sure but with some help finding a place to start, four was soon written and objects found.

As you continued, we worked together to find starting points for writing numbers and you were quick to find objects to match the number. You used your finger to count the objects as the groups got larger. As the number writing went higher you used counting skills to recheck which number was the next number to write.

What did I learn about you today?

Blake, you did an awesome job today. You showed me that you have developed a strong understanding about numerals, one-to-one correspondence, forming sets/classification and exploring numeral sequences. 'Numbers' or numerals play a big part in young children's lives. On a daily basis they are exposed to a variety of numerals, from road signs to price tags, from pictures in books to images on television or the iPad.

The more young children play with numerals the more confident they will be at using them in their play and everyday interactions. The concept of one-to-one correspondence requires an understanding that each object being counted represents one more and is important because the understanding attached to counting is a key idea on which all other number concepts are based(NZMaths.co.nz).

Blake you also showed me how you can use your working knowledge about numbers to help you solve number problems or challenges.

It has been great seeing your mathematic interest building over the month and it has been supported by your strong literacy interest.

Where to next?

Maybe we could try exploring measuring or geometric shape exploration tied in with your numeral interest next?

Kaiako: Sarah G

Learning Story 3.5 *One-to-one correspondence*

Author: Sharon Garrod

as he went along, and this was an additional motivation to be willing to persevere with this number work. An added comment says that this engagement with numbers (writing them down) has been supported by his 'strong literacy interest'. Both aspects of being willing are illustrated here: this task continued an interest for him, and being prepared to persevere was enhanced by the camera.

Elsie is a pattern maker!

One way to detect a motivation is to notice, recognise and respond to an initiative from the child. In Learning Story 3.6, 'Elsie is a pattern maker!', Elsie, an 18-month-old child, is initiating a knocking-on-the-window patterning game with the early childhood teacher. She gets very excited when the teacher repeats the pattern that she introduces. She is 'not amused' when the teacher 'makes a mistake'. This is an example of Elsie being inclined or 'ready' to engage in this game; it is also an example of spontaneous mathematics. A mathematics researcher from the University of Canterbury, Jane McChesney, writes (for us) that the following are examples of patterning in early mathematics: noticing a pattern; being sensitive to pattern; a focus on the order of a pattern and recognising repeated elements; making, generating, altering, extending, predicting, echoing a pattern; being able to 'repair' a pattern. Elsie was certainly engaging in early mathematics: being ready and able to engage in patterning. Furthermore, the teacher's enthusiastic response enabled her to be willing to initiate and pursue this game.

Spencer helps out

Learning Story 3.7, 'Spencer helps out', is written at Spencer's childcare centre. He is ready/inclined to assist caring for the younger children. Furthermore, this centre has a whānau (extended family) centre environment, in which children of all ages play and work together, so the environment enables him (he is willing to) help out with the younger children. The teacher identifies the on-going learning when she writes to Spencer in the Learning Story, 'Spencer, in your portfolio there is a similar story by Karen, about you caring for the babies when you were a toddler'. The comment, 'Without a word being said, up you jumped, eager to lend a hand' identifies his readiness to take responsibility for others, able to be actioned in this multi-age environment. Note that this Learning Story also adds a powerful framing (the topic of Chapter 4), which places this caring disposition in a wider cultural frame: 'Through these interactions', the teacher writes, 'you are exploring and deepening your knowledge around the important values of Tikanga Māori, and the importance of living in a community that cares for each other'.

Akari's challenge !!!!

In Learning Story 3.8, 'Akari's challenge', a succession of ten photographs record the many times that Akari challenged herself to climb a climbing wall. Another child gives her a hand, and the title of the Learning Story includes four exclamation

Elsie is a Pattern Maker!

Kia ora koe Elsie
I have been noticing your interest in the pattern making concepts that you recognise in your everyday life. You love to dance and your favourite songs are repeating action songs like *Heads, Shoulders Knees and Toes.* You also often try to initiate 'up, down, up!' games with your friends and kaiako at kindy. But, one of your most favourite things to do is knock on the window. You will knock once, put your hands in the air and then knock two or three times. I now copy this action and you get very excited. We often repeat this game over and over again, sometimes I play a trick on you and knock a different number of times and you will stop, then start your knocking pattern again. Not amused!

What learning do I think is happening here?
Elsie, you are developing your mathematical reasoning in the every day moments of your life. You communicate this by showing your amusement and delight, and by engaging others in many different pattern making moments.

How might we stretch your learning?
I can help support your learning by acknowledging and talking to you about the patterns that you identify in your routines and adventures. Tino pai rawa atu Elsie, I think that this is just the beginning of your life long love of mathematical learning!
Ngā mihi nui
Written by
Becs

Learning Story 3.6 *Elsie is a pattern maker!*

Author: Rebecca Thomas

Spencer Helps Out

Spencer, it warms my heart to see how thoughtful and caring your are with our younger children. I often see you passing them an object you think they might be interested in, giving them a reassuring hug or helping them out in small ways that let them know they are important, that they are loved. Today, at the kai table, you saw that Alice was asking for her zip lock bag to be opened. Without a word being said, up you jumped eager to lend a hand. Then, before you sat down to finish your kai, you pushed Sienna's chair in for her.

What learning do I see happening here?

Spencer, in your portfolio there is a similar story by Karen, about you caring for the babies when you were a toddler. Clearly you are imitating the care and nurturing you have received from your whānau. Perhaps you have also seen your mum in action caring for others in her workplace?

Ehara taku toa I te toa takitahi engari he toa takitini. I come not with my own strengths but bring with me the gifts, talents and strengths of my family, tribe and ancestors.

Being involved in a whānau centre environment like this gives you more opportunities to see responsive and positive relationships between young and old. This helps to support your understanding about babies and how we interact with them. Through modelling and respectful practice, empathy can be fostered and nurtured. Spencer, we see that you are finding new ways to show aroha and take responsibility for others. Through these kinds of interactions you are exploring and deepening your knowledge around the important values of Tikanga Māori, and the importance of living in a community that cares for each other.

Where might this learning lead to next?

Our younger children learn by watching and listening to big children like you Spencer. Conversely, there are many ways you can extend your learning alongside them. You can practise your leadership skills and cement your learning by teaching them how to do new things. You might also be inspired by our younger children to engage in activities that build your creativity. I know you have some great story ideas. Would you like to tell a story next time you sit with us?

Written for you by Bridget

Learning Story 3.7 *Spencer helps out*

Author: Bridget O'Connor

Akari's Challenge!!!!

Akari challenged herself to climb the board over and over again.

It is difficult to reach the top of the board but finally, with the help of her friends, she could climb there.

Akari challenged herself to climb the board over and over again.

It is difficult to reach the top of the board but finally, with the help of her friends, she could climb there.

Learning Story 3.8 *Akari's challenge*
Author: Yuka Sato

marks. This is another example of enabling children to read their own Learning Story. Apart from having it read to them several times, so that they might memorise it, in this case the photos and the exclamation marks invoke the excitement the writer of the story feels at Akari's final success.

The hopes and dreams of new parents: an enabling society and world

We include the following as an example of new parents being 'sensitive to occasion' in their aspirations for their newborns. In a longitudinal study of New Zealand children and their families, *Growing Up in New Zealand*, 6,822 pregnant women were recruited in 2009–2010, and agreed to their children's participation. Report One was published in 2010: *Growing Up in New Zealand: Before We Are Born* (Morton et al., 2010). This report provides detailed information gathered from face-to-face interviews with the recruited mothers (and the fathers) of the child cohort, from the first antenatal data collection wave. The Growing Up in New Zealand child cohort of 6,846 babies is explicitly designed to provide relevant and robust evidence for an analysis of the growing up of a representative group of New Zealanders. Approximately one in four children are identified as Māori, one in five children identified within the broad Pacific ethnic group, and one in six within the Asian ethnic group. One in three of the cohort children was born to at least one parent who did not grow up in New Zealand themselves.

A component of this longitudinal study included asking prospective parents, during pregnancy, about their hopes and dreams for their children. Parents expressed a hope that their children would contribute to their local community and to New Zealand more generally, so that the world would be a better place for their being in it. *These aspirations for their own children were also accompanied by a parallel hope that the society and world their children would grow up in would enable this contribution* (our italics).

To summarise, an assessment of an outcome is not fair if the opportunity to learn (the OTL) that outcome is not enabled, encouraged or welcomed in the relevant community of practice.

This means that a learning disposition is not just an individual matter, it is the learner *plus a facilitating environment*. This is important. A collaborative environment can enhance individual ability, as Melissa Gresalfi (2009: 362) emphasises when she concludes from her research in school mathematics classes that: 'collaboration creates opportunities for students to engage more deeply with mathematical content than they might have done on their own'.

This chapter reflects the sociocultural nature of a Learning Story assessment, and the following quote comes from a chapter entitled 'A sociocultural perspective on opportunity to learn' in an edited book entirely devoted to issues of assessment, equity and opportunity to learn. James Paul Gee says:

Ensuring that all learners have had an equal OTL is both an ethical prerequisite for fair assessment and a solid base on which to think about educational reforms that will ensure that all children can succeed at school. (Gee in Moss et al., 2008: 76)

What might a learning environment in an early childhood centre or a school classroom that enables and encourages learning dispositions look like?

We suggest that portfolios of Learning Stories, describing examples of the learner's approach to novel problems, persistence in the face of challenge, and interactions with others – or any other combination of learning dispositions valued here – would be one way of representing such an environment.

Photo 3.1 *Learning portfolios in an early childhood environment*

Further thinking

1. Do you have a story that is similar to Carol Dweck's and Vivian Paley's early stories in which they felt that an environment or a curriculum made them feel reluctant to improvise, critique and initiate a learning task?
2. What learning dispositions (or learning habits) do you use on many occasions? Are some of them positive (helpful), and are some of them negative (unhelpful)? Where are the situations in which you readily apply them?
3. Could you expand the list of the situations for the helpful learning dispositions? How might you begin to do that?
4. What learning dispositions would you like to acquire or strengthen? Are they available for you, where you work, play or live?

Further reading

Carr, Margaret and Lee, Wendy (2012) *Learning Stories: Constructing Learner Identities in Early Education*. London: SAGE. Chapter 7: Reconceptualising assessment.

New Zealand Ministry of Education (2004) *Kei tua o te Pae* Book 6 – *Assessment and Learning: Competence*. Downloadable at: www.education.govt.nz/assets/Documents/Early-Childhood/Kei-Tua-o-te-Pae/ECEBooklet6Full.pdf (accessed 3 December 2018).

Note

1. A 'hopper' is a funnel-shaped reservoir for feeding grain (for instance) into a railway truck.

Ngā mihi nui = Thank you very much. Or kind regards (with more emphasis on gratitude)

Whānau = Extended family, multigenerational group of relatives or group of people who work together on and for a common cause

Tikanga = Correct procedure, custom, lore, way, code, meaning, practice, convention - the customary system of values and practices that have developed over time and are deeply embedded in the social context

Kai = Food, meal

Tino pai rawa atu = Excellent!

4

Recognising Powerful Frameworks

Expert learning needs expert teachers, and to become expert teachers we need to be expert learners ourselves. So the book's *The Expert Learner* title is deliberately ambiguous: it's about both the learner and the teacher. As in other professions, teaching expertise is the product of using experience to develop *powerful frameworks* in which to make sense of both familiar and unfamiliar information. (Gordon Stobart, 2014: 14; our emphasis)

It is through narrative that we create and re-create selfhood, and self is a product of our telling and re-telling. We are, from the start, expressions of our culture. Culture is replete with alternative narratives about what self is or might be. (Jerome Bruner, 2003: 86)

Key messages

- Powerful frameworks will shape assessment
- Assessments will construct a learner self
- Revisiting and retelling Learning Stories creates and confirms a powerful framework

Teacher question: What do we look for when we write a Learning Story?

Powerful frameworks will shape assessment

We argued in Chapter 3 that if an assessment is to be fair, then it must (i) attend to the notion of a person-plus, (ii) take account of whether the learner is unwilling to risk pursuing an outcome because the resources are not available and the culture of the context appears unsympathetic, and (iii) recognise that positive affect enhances the opportunity to learn. These are requirements for an assessment regime that is just and equitable.

We also recognise that assessments in early childhood education contexts and in schools have meaning if they implicitly or explicitly connect to a powerful framework or Big Picture vision that learners, teachers and families can understand. A powerful framework in this context might also be called a 'script for action'. It is central to formative assessments.

Assessing across two levels

Formative assessments assess across two levels: they assess the pieces, while explicitly or implicitly referencing a Big Picture vision. The powerful frameworks in education can also be called the 'big narratives'; in practice they are made up from small stories, as Jerome Bruner (2003) reminds us. We might see it as a mosaic, and the stories we tell as mosaic pieces that can be fitted into the frame, in different ways, for different contexts and different learners. For instance, there is no one route to becoming a confident mathematician. The example of Elsie in Chapter 3 was a case in point. Her teacher recognised that the fun 'knocking on the window' game that 18 month-old Elsie had devised was developing a pattern-based 'conversation', and that this pattern-making routine was also an example of early mathematics. During discussions with a researcher, this teacher was beginning to think of other ways in which Elsie might become engrossed in pattern-making 'conversations'; the early childhood centre was full of opportunities, including musical instruments like drums and xylophones, wooden mosaic shapes, and blocks. Mathematics was also the powerful framework for the assessment of Blake's interest in numbers in Chapter 3. There are also a number of ways to become a confident reader; the boys reading their portfolios with each other was one piece of that big picture (learning to read); teachers and families revisiting Learning Stories with children is another. Learning Stories about the self are engaging; they add that central element for learning, emotion. In Learning Story 4.1, Ashlyn, a very young child, not yet walking, is mimicking a cadence of reading aloud because she loves being read to.

A story reading performer

The photo for Learning Story 4.1, 'A story reading performer', comes from a video of Ashlyn, 'singing' in a rhythmic story-reading style as she turns the pages. She has been an avid listener to stories for some time, and her parent reports that she 'can't get enough of people reading to her'. In terms of being ready, willing and able to be a reader, the teacher comments too on her ability: she understands that print contains a message, that story can be full of drama, and the video shows her turning the pages in sequence with the rhythm. The teacher takes a wide lens on this story, describing it as part of a powerful framework of 'languages': ICT, art, dance and music, all available here for the children to experience. We return to this idea in Chapter 8 where we re-frame 'preparation for school' as constructing an expanded repertoire of languages for possibility thinking and ways of making sense of the world.

Courage

Learning Story 4.2, 'Courage', is written for Hannah by a Hospital Play Specialist. She refers back to an earlier visit, to frame a big picture of Hannah as including 'the ability to take responsibility, being involved in aspects of your care and expressing your opinions'. This time the powerful frame is *courage*: strength in the face of difficulty, and resilience. The eloquent photo of Hannah with play dough illustrates this frame. Sue, the writer of the story, emphasises that while courage is really helpful now, this disposition 'will be helpful as you grow and continue your learning journey'. She defines this learning disposition further, as a way to approach learning opportunities: persisting with challenge and difficulty, and children and adults taking risks to extend themselves. This is a story from New Zealand, and the writer finishes it with a Māori whakataukī, a proverb, Kia maia te āwhā tū maiaitia he ua, translated as *Brave the storm and dance in the rain*.

A national curriculum

Most countries have a national early childhood curriculum, in addition to a school one, constructed to provide a national cultural framework about a learner self.

A story reading performer

Watching Ashlyn read is like watching an artist perform!

I felt so privileged to see Ashlyn so avidly reading to herself and it struck me that this was all about the kind of passion and engagement that keeps learners coming back to a burning interest. It was an intrinsic reward that was driving her repeated adventures with books. When I had a chat with Freya it seems that Ashlyn can't get enough of people reading to her. Just looking at her style I'd say that she is imitating some very vibrant readers. What fabulous models they've been, as her desire to involve herself in books has been cemented by those around her attentively listening to this interest and widening and deepening her experiences.

My thoughts on Ashlyn's learning...

Now, in our learning community here at Greerton, she is also having plenty of practice. We have so many books available and so much meaningful print on our walls associated with our children's interests that Ashlyn is immersed in literacy in its widest sense. Add the way we wrap ICT, art, dance and music around each child's interests, then we have many 'languages' for children to express themselves and explore their world. I have often seen Ashlyn in full 'reading mode'. The way she

Ashlyn is a dispositional reader meaning she has the motivation to keep deepening and widening her literacy experiences.

responds to books tells us all that she understands print conveys a message, that story is full of drama, and that she has practised many of the nuances that reading orally requires. She has sentence structure 'off pat' with the way she uses intonation in her voice to show the beginning and end. I can't help thinking that Ashlyn has already developed many of the skills that underpin independent readers' ability to decode print effectively.

How might we all grow this learning together?

We all, of course will continue encouraging this love of literacy; of story, of drama, in many and varied ways, so her love of these continues to flourish. It is that burning desire that will motivate her continued exploration and grow it further as she continues to lead her own learning in supportive environments both here and at home. Arohanui Lorraine

Learning Story 4.1 *A story reading performer*
Author: Lorraine Sands

Courage

Nā Sue – Hospital Play Specialist

Kia ora Hannah!
It seems so long since I last saw you and your lovely family here in the children's ward. When I last saw you I was struck by your ability to take responsibility, being involved in aspects of your care and expressing your opinions. This time it is courage that comes to mind when I see you and spend some time with you. Courage is about strength in the face of difficulty. Hannah, I see you approach the many challenges you face with great courage. Being courageous doesn't mean you aren't ever scared, or find some situations a bit scary. I notice that when things are tough you are strong and resilient Hannah. This is courage.

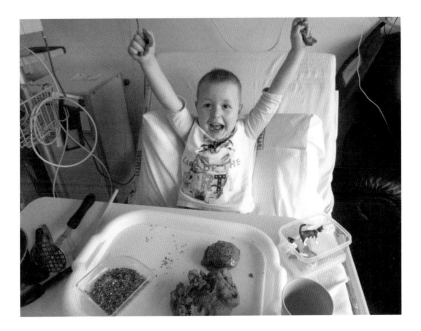

Look at this face and posture Hannah! Resilience means you 'bounce' back and continue to find joy in the things you love to do. Mum says you love playdough, how fabulous there was some waiting for you when you arrived today!

Being courageous is really helpful for you while you are having times in hospital Hannah, but will also be really helpful for you as you grow and continue your learning journey. Children and adults who approach learning opportunities with courage, are more likely to persist with challenge and difficulty, and take risks to extend themselves.
You will have many more opportunities to practise and continue to grow a courageous attitude Hannah. I look forward to watching this unfold for you with the support of your family.

Kia maia te āwhā tū maiangitia he ua
Brave the storm and dance in the rain

Learning Story 4.2 *Courage*

Author: Sue Fahey

New Zealand's early childhood curriculum (*Te Whāriki*) provides an example. It was developed in 1996, and revised in 2017 (see *Understanding the Te Whāriki Approach*: Lee, Carr, Soutar and Mitchell, 2013; also *Weaving Te Whāriki*: Gunn and Nuttall, 2019). This bicultural and bilingual curriculum is built on the metaphor of a whāriki, a weaving of a mat from many strands. The 2017 update of this national curriculum is in a 'flip' design; the curriculum is in both English and te reo Māori (the indigenous Māori language) and neither is placed first. When the document is opened at the place where the two parts of the flip book meet, it can be seen that the whāriki is unfinished, with loose strands still to be woven. This acknowledges the child's potential and their ongoing educational journey (New Zealand MoE, 2017, Inside Cover).

The initial framing of this weaving is provided by four principles: in English they are Empowerment, Holistic development, Family and community, and Relationships. The curriculum states:

> Perspectives on empowerment are culturally located, hence kaiako [teachers] need to seek the input of children and their parents and whānau [extended family] when designing the local curriculum. (New Zealand MoE, 2017: 18)

One of five strands of outcome that follows from the principles is Communication/Mana reo: *The languages and symbols of children's own and other countries are promoted and protected*. That strand includes the following two of five learning outcomes: 'Understanding oral language and using it for a range of purposes', and 'Recognising mathematical symbols and concepts and using them with enjoyment, meaning and purpose'. Elsie and Blake's Learning Stories in Chapter 3 exemplified those mathematics outcomes.

This is a story from New Zealand. It is a narrative assessment written in te reo Māori (Māori language) from a kōhanga reo, one of many early childhood centres where only te reo Māori is spoken. It includes a whakataukī (proverb) that recognises the powerful framework of te reo Māori. It has been translated into English for this book.

He Kaikōrero Māori/A Māori language speaker

This paki ako (Learning Story 4.3, 'He Kaikōrero Māori/A Māori language speaker') documents and praises the growth in language expertise for a young child, Te Ao Tuhi i te Rangi; it references powerful frameworks and metaphors. The kaiako, Leanne, summarises the development by referring to two occasions in the past: looking back to 'last year' when the three useful words (anei, tenei, panana) were noted. She comments on progress made during the holiday 'you filled your basket with new words'. Leanne then describes recent (this morning) examples: purposeful te reo Māori used in longer sentences. The kaiako enriches the story in a cultural way by using the metaphor of birdsong (the kaka and the kōkō) to express and illustrate her admiration. She acknowledges both the child and the whānau (family) for their commitment to speak the Māori language. Finally, the story ends with a whakataukī.

He Kaikōrero Māori

Te Ao Tuhi o Hiwa i te rangi, nei te reo uruhau e whakamiha atu nei ki a koe me tō arero Māori.

I tērā tau, i a koe e pakupaku tonu ana i timata ai te whakahua i ngā kupu Māori, ko te 'anei', 'tēnei' me te 'panana' ngā tino kupu i kōrerohia.

Heoi anō, i roto i ngā hararei i whakakīkī tō kete kupu ki ngā kupu hou, ā, kua hoki mai koe he manu kākā e ketekete ana i tō taenga mai, tae atu ki tō hokinga ki te kainga.

Nō te ata tonu nei, ka omaoma atu koe ki waho e karanga ana, "Paihikara, paihikara". Ka kake koe i te paihikara parahutihuti ana te haere, kātahi nā ka raruraru tō wīra ki te ara.

"Mau, mau, mau", tāu i korero mai.

"Āe, kua mau tō wīra" tāku ki a koe.

Heke iho koe i te paihikara ka mea, "Kua mau, kua mau! Pana! Pana! Pana paihikara!"

Ka panaia te paihikara kia tika te noho a te wīra ki te ara me te mea ake, "Arā!"

E mihi ana ki tō whakarongo pīkari. Ka mutu, he kōrero Māori anō nei he kākā haetara.

Mīharo mārika nei ahau ki te mātakitaki i a koe e whanake nei, e mārama kehokeho nei ki tō ao, ki tō reo anō hoki.

Nā reira e te kākā haetara, e te kōkō takakī, nei te mihi maioha ki a koutou ko tō whānau e ū hītararī tonu ana ki te korero i te reo Māori.

Ko te reo te mauri o te mana Māori!

Nā Pou Leanne

Learning Story 4.3 *He Kakōrero Māori / A Māori language speaker (part 1)*
Author: Leanne Clayton

A Māori Language Speaker

Te Ao Tuhi o Hiwa i te rangi, here is the pleasing response of admiration for you and your native tongue.

Last year, while you were still very young, you began to express these Māori words regularly 'anei' (here it is), 'tēnei' (this) and 'panana' (banana).

Then, during your holiday you filled your basket with new words and returned like a kākā (native parrot) bird full of constant chatter on arrival until you left for home at the end of the day.

It was only this morning when you ran outside calling, "Paihikara, paihikara" (Bicycle, bicycle). You climbed on the bike and sped off, but then your wheel was a challenge on the path.

"Mau, mau, mau" (Stuck, stuck, stuck), you said.

"Āe, kua mau tō wīra" (Yes, your wheel is stuck), I responded to you.

You got off you bike and said, "Kua mau, kua mau! Pana! Pana! Pana paihikara!" (It's stuck, it's stuck! Push! Push! Push bike!)

You pushed the bike so that the wheel sat correctly and then said, "Arā!" (That's it!)

I want to acknowledge you as a careful listener. The result, you speak Māori just like the admired kākā bird.

I am filled with wonder observing you developing, how deeply you understand your world and your native tongue.

Therefore admired kākā bird, eloquent kōkō (parson bird), this is my affectionate acknowledgement to you and your whānau for your commitment to speak the Māori language.

Ko te reo te mauri o te mana Māori! (The language is the life essence of Māori existence)

Written by Pou Leanne

Learning Story 4.3 *He Kakōrero Māori / A Māori language speaker (part 2)*
Author: Leanne Clayton

Children revisiting and retelling Learning Stories

We have so far included many examples of teachers noticing, recognising and recording a Learning Story. In Chapter 1 we included a story of children revisiting their Stories. This is a common happening, especially when the portfolios are readily available. The revisiting with a teacher reminds them of the formative purpose: how they might progress this learning. It also assists them to begin to recognise the wider learning framework for which the latest story is a part, as the following comment by Delwyn during a research project illustrates:

> *Delwyn (teacher) is revisiting Andrew's portfolio of Learning Stories with him.*

> Andrew (commenting on a new Learning Story he hasn't seen before): Is that me doing my book?

> Teacher: Yes, when you were becoming an author.

In a similar context (reading), David Perkins, in his 2009 book entitled *Making Learning Whole*, points out that:

> First and most important, children and adults learning to swim, no matter what they themselves can do, have a sense of what the whole performance looks like. They see swimmers cruising back and forth all the time. Compare this with children in the third grade studying arithmetic, who typically have no clue about what maths is really for, even in junior versions. [...] Seen in this way, whole-game undertakings like careful listening to and discussion about a story should be considered work on the larger enterprise of reading. (Perkins, 2009a: 40, 41)

In Chapter 3 we referred to research findings which indicate that if children become proficient and confident in telling and retelling stories during their early years, they are more likely to become competent readers at an early age.

My learner identity

Learning Story 4.4, 'My learner identity', begins when Tong Tong asks, 'Can you show me how to write a story?', the teacher realises she means the Learning Stories in the portfolio books. She shows Tong Tong how she takes photos of learning activities, and teaches her how to use the camera. Another child joins in, and takes photographs of Tong Tong taking photographs. Then the story writing begins, with Tong Tong dictating. The teacher noted that this was not the first time Tong Tong had shown an interest in documenting her own learning. To grow the learning further she suggests that they explore some of the Māori legends that are similar to those from China, reminding her of one of them.

My learner identity

Written by Rachel with aroha alongside Tong Tong Zheng

Tong Tong, when I was a young girl I had a book about mermaids that was very special to me. I used to read it often and can still remember being totally absorbed in the beautiful illustrations. I remembered this story when you brought in your book *Rupert the Bear and the Mermaids*, and were inspired to make that mermaid tail and build a mermaid castle. I wrote a story about that for you and in that story I said that I would find a copy of the book I had as a child to show to you.

I brought the book outside one day to share the story with you. I observed you as you carefully studied the cover.

'I like mermaids,' you said,'I like Ariel'.
Tong Tong, you have shared your love for Ariel and the other Disney Princesses with me many times. You told me that you have a book with all the princesses in it at home. We opened the book and I started to read it to you.
'This castle is just like Ariel's,' you commented.
The mermaid in the story has a dolphin friend who she rides.
'Ariel has friends like this, too,' you told me. I remember Ariel is friends with a crab named Sebastian and a fish called Flounder.

I remember a few days ago we were talking on the swings. You turned to me and said,'I have a good idea. Whaihanga needs a tree'.
I pointed at our big tree by the carpentry table, but you shook your head.
'No, Whaihanga needs a tree where you can sit'.
I understood that desire; we are unable to climb the tree we have here because the branches are up very high, and the tree is over concrete. You went and shared your idea with some of the other teachers and children.
The next day, while we were talking on the swings in the evening, you said to me, 'What is Neko's rabbit's name?'
'Rufus,' I told you.You started to laugh.
'I want a rabbit. I would name it Goldie'. I told you I thought that was a lovely name.
'I have lots of good ideas,'you said with a confident smile.'I have good ideas about trees, about names, about sleeping, about my body'.
After some more thinking you asked, 'Can you show me how to write a story?'

Through conversation I realised you meant stories that go into our portfolio books. You have shown a strong interest in your own book since you first started coming to Whaihanga. You often ask me to write more stories for your book, and show me the empty pages, asking that I fill them! You even wondered why I myself don't have a book, and said that I could get Whaea Jo to write stories for me in one. Today I took my camera out and showed you how I use it to write stories. I told you that you could use my camera to take photos of something special to you, or something that interested you, or something that you would like to write about. I showed you which buttons to press to turn the camera on and off, and how to view photos that you had taken. You looped the strap around your wrist and went purposefully over to the books.

'I want Mountain of Fire and We're Going on a Bear Hunt,' you said.

Angie, inspired by you, wanted to take photos too. She captured the following photos of you as you took photos of the story.

Below are the photographs that you took yourself

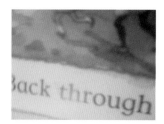

Learning Story 4.4   *My learner identity (part 1)*
Author: Rachel Chambers-Field

When you had finished, you brought the camera out to me. You were also carrying We're Going on a Bear Hunt.
'I took photos of this page and this page and the bear,' you told me, showing me each page in the book that
you had photographed.
'Now, show me how to write the story,' you told me.
We went and found some paper and pens. I told you that I would record your words and to tell me whatever was
important to you.
'The Mountain of Fire,' you began, 'he will turn to ice'.
You stopped for a moment and looked at me,
'How do you make fire hot?'
I commented that was an excellent question that got me thinking.
You then moved on to explaining the next photos you had taken.
'We're going on a bear hunt, we're going to catch a big one. What a beautiful day! We're not scared'.
Tong Tong added her own writing to the bottom of the page.
'Oh,' you continued,' his sisters are very warm'.

Tong Tong was curious about the next step.
'I will write the words we have written here on the computer, and print out the photos you have taken. Then we can put
it in your book,' I explained.
'How do you print?' Tong Tong asked.
I showed Tong Tong the SD card inside the camera and how to take it out.
'The photos are in here,' I said, 'and I put it into the computer. I use the computer to print them from the printer.'
Tong Tong seemed satisfied with this answer and smiled.

What learning could be happening here for Tong Tong?

Tong Tong, this is not the first time you have shown an interest in creating your own documentation. A few weeks ago you
drew a picture and asked that I photograph you with it for your portfolio book. You take pride in all the stories about your
learning journey in your portfolio and desire to add to them.

Tong Tong, when I suggested you could take photographs of something special to you, I was not surprised to see you
choose books, especially a Māori legend. You continue to show a deep appreciation for these stories. We're Going on a Bear
Hunt has also been a special book to you for some time, and features in stories in your portfolio.

Tong Tong, another thing that stands out for me is how strong your identity as a learner is. You recognise that you have 'good
ideas' and want to share those ideas with others. You recognise your own power, your mana, and creativity. I remember not
long ago, I was watching you climbing on the playground.

'I have strong legs, strong bottom, and strong arms,' you told me, flexing your arm muscles at me. You continued to climb
with complete confidence in your ability.

You have such a strong perception of yourself!

How could this learning grow from here?

I have been fascinated with your deep interest in Māori legends for a while now. Whaea Michelle showed me an interesting
article in a magazine, written by a woman named Song Lam, about the similarities between Māori and Chinese cultures.
She writes that there are similarities in the legends and folktales of both of these cultures, likening Maui to Sun Wu Kong
(the Monkey King). I wonder Tong Tong, if you know any of the stories about him? I would love to read some of them. In
Chinese legend, there is also a woman called Chang E, who lives alone on the moon. Doesn't this remind you of the story
of Rona and the Moon that we have read so many times? I wonder what learning might happen if we looked into these stories?

Tong Tong, I am so enjoying journeying alongside you as you develop your ideas. You are a creative and deep thinker,
Tong Tong – and the best thing is, you know it!

Learning Story 4.4 *My learner identity (part 2)*

Author: Rachel Chambers-Field

Assessments will construct a learner self

Gordon Stobart comments that one of the main themes of his book, *Testing Times: The Uses and Abuses of Assessment* (Stobart, 2008: 6), is that *assessment shapes who and what we are and cannot be treated as a neutral measure of abilities or skills that are independent of society*. Identities are shaped by how people are assessed, labelled and sorted by society, and especially by education. The comment from Jerome Bruner about the power of story that began this chapter reminds us that, by extension, a portfolio of Learning Stories can construct a learner self. A good example of the way that a specific assessment can create and re-create a learner self is the attached Learning Story from China: 'Dad, me and the spider'.

Dad, me and the spider

Learning Story 4.5, 'Dad, me and the spider', begins when Huang draws on the wall of the sleep-room at the childcare centre, and the children complain. The teacher here had several choices to respond to this situation, and then to write it up as a Learning Story. She chose to recognise this as an example of imagination, possibly representing a significant image for the child. Further conversation with Huang confirmed this. The Learning Story describes Huang as a positive learner self, an artist who creates from the heart. Suggesting that colour could be added to the black and white picture, plus the talk that accompanied this and the Learning Story that reified the event, enabled the teacher and the child to co-construct a different narrative from the initial complaint. There is some connection here to the Reggio Emilia philosophy (see Rinaldi, 2006), which flows from the early years into the high school, and the multimodal is foregrounded to vividly illustrate and represent the children's ideas and feelings. Perhaps we could say that – in the words of Gunilla Dahlberg in the Foreword to the *Loris Malaguzzi and the Schools of Reggio Emilia* (Cagliari et al., 2016: xi) – this is an example of 'setting ethics and aesthetics in motion' (2016: xi), leaving the authors of this Learning Story (including the painter) with a 'new serenity and responsibility'.

Revisiting and retelling Learning Stories creates and confirms a powerful framework

A vivid example of the power of Learning Stories is provided in the book written by kindergarten teachers and researchers about their policies and practices for the children transitioning to school: *Crossing the Border: A Community Negotiates the Transition from Early Childhood to School* (Hartley et al., 2012). In Chapter 9 of that book, the authors emphasise the links between early childhood and the

Dad, Me and Spider

By Wei Feng

During the last few days, some children kept complaining to me that somebody had drawn on the wall. Today, the children complained again.

I asked, "Where is it?"

The children took me to the sleep-room. They told me, "Huang did it".

You quietly stood behind the door of the sleep-room, not saying a word.

I said to you, "Do not worry. Tell me what have you drawn?"

You whispered to me, "This is Dad (the big figure), this is me (the small figure), we are looking at a spider (the black figure on the top)".

I asked, "What were you thinking about while drawing?"

You said, "I like to be with Dad, but Dad is so busy".

"Do you want to see this picture more often?" I asked.

"Yes". You nodded your head.

I then brought over some paints and suggested you and I could add some colours to your drawing.

You were very surprised with my suggestion, and I could also feel your great excitement. You like blue, so we put blue on you and your dad's clothes.

Since then, I often see you standing in front of this painting, touching it, looking at it and protecting it. So I decided to write about this, to let your dad see it.

Learning Story 4.5 *Dad, me and spider*

Author: Wei Feng

school curriculum, and then they analyse the Learning Stories by 'noticing, recognising and recording' the learning in one of the children's kindergarten books (portfolios of Learning Stories). They identify the development of Cree's learner identity by focusing on the school curriculum's definition of a learner self identified in five dispositional key competencies (Thinking; Using language, symbols and texts; Managing self; Relating to others; and Participating and contributing). Hartley et al. comment that the Learning Stories reveal that Cree is already a 'confident, connected, actively involved learner' (2012: 87).

Kaitiaki of Papatūānuku – exploring and caring

The translation of the title of Learning Story 4.6, 'Kaitiaki of Papatūānuku', is guardian/caretaker of Mother Earth. It celebrates young SJ's caring, exploring and curiosity in the context of a collaborative venture with an older child to construct an enclosure to look after little frogs. The teacher analyses this learning in terms of exploration, curiosity, taking an interest in the environment, problem-solving and 'soaking up meaning from the people around you'. SJ's engagement with this task was evident when he showed his mum and dad the frog enclosure. The photograph with Matariki illustrates his concentration while holding the food for the tiger worms, and the story affectionately describes him running away when they were fed. The 'What next?' is nicely labelled 'Growing your learning further', and specific: inviting SJ to assist with feeding the tiger worms on another occasion, and promising to support further explorations. This story celebrates SJ's caring, and the sub-text of the 'Growing your learning further' section is to construct or re-construct his learner self as 'about to become brave'. This learner self will be revisited and re-told.

Waiting for Dad on this side of the border

A different account of retelling a story, with a very different kind of border at the heart of the story, is illustrated in Zahid's portfolio as the teachers contribute to his initiatives to construct some meaning of his father's absence as a detained immigrant. This Learning Story was translated from the child's home language. In his first Learning Story 4.7, 'Waiting for Dad on this side of the border', the teachers assist Zahid to draw his father's journey from Mexico on a map, enabling him to draw a strong line to represent the border between Mexico and California. In this first story, in a section entitled 'What activities could we plan to support you in exploring this topic that you are so interested in?' they invite him to represent his ideas and feelings with paint strokes and acrylic colours. This provokes the second story. In the first story they invite a comment from the family, and the mother replies.

> Zahid is not very fond of writing, but he talks a lot and also understands quite a lot. He doesn't like drawing but maybe with your support here at school he could find enjoyment in drawing or painting.

Under the same sun

In Zahid's second Learning Story 4.8, 'Under the same sun', the teacher writes an encouraging comment on this new mode of expressing his feelings:

Kaitiaki of Papatūānuku – exploring and caring

Learning and growth happen in every moment of every day; you cannot have play and exploration without learning, they are completely interconnected!

SJ, you have such a curiosity about each and every thing at Whaihanga. This curiosity takes us from the sandpit, the paints, the puzzles, to the worm farm, the climbing obstacles, the kai table, and everywhere else inbetween. Recently we walked past the frog enclosure and you asked about it. With this prompt, I opened up the lid and we started the frog hunt. Where could our frogs be? We talked about how they are hibernating at the moment with the chilly winter and spring weather. They do not need food now, and try to move as little as possible to not use much energy. After gently lifting up the rocks and branch, we found the brown frog under the water dish, and the green one nestled in the grass plant. You were very interested, SJ, and repeated back "frog" to me as you pointed and observed this little frog. After changing the bowl of water in their environment, we headed off to our next moment of being kaitiaki/caretakers of our precious Papatūānuku.

Matariki went to get the kai for the worms from the kitchen, with you beside her. She handed you the kai, and together you came out to the worm farm. This was your first time seeing our worm farm in action, and I sensed your uncertainty and hesitation. I came close and stood beside you, and with encouragement you stood up to look inside. Matariki tipped the kai into the worm bin and you ran away as fast as you could! I smiled, SJ, and recognised how new this was for you. Kai pai for the courage and curiosity it took to approach and peek in to the wriggling tiger worms.

My thoughts on your learning

SJ, each day you immerse yourself in exploring and learning. Your curiosity sparks an interest, and by following what interests you, you are naturally leading your own learning. Exploring and taking an interest in your environment is important as you learn and think about your world, experiment, problem solve and soak up meaning from the people around you.

I smiled when Mum Zoey and Dad Francis came to pick you up and you showed them the frog enclosure. This moment of frog hunting we shared together was important to you, and to share this with your whānau is very special.

Growing your learning further

I wonder if you would like to join us next time we feed the tiger worms, SJ? I know without a doubt that you will continue to explore and show me where you would like to lead your learning next! Written by Alysha Fraser

Learning Story 4.6 *Kaitiaki of Papatūānuku – exploring and caring*

Author: Alysha Fraser

Waiting for Dad on this side of the border

Isauro M. Escamilla

What happened? What's the story?

Zahid, I admire your initiative to tell us the tale of the travels your dad has undertaken to reunite with you and your family in California. On a map you showed us Mexico City where you say your dad started his journey to the North. You spoke about the border (la frontera) and you asked us to help you find Nebraska and Texas on our map, because that's where you say your dad was detained. We asked you, *What is the border?* and you answered: *"It is a place where they arrest you because you are an immigrant. My dad was detained because he wanted to go to California to be with me".*

What is the significance of this story?

Zahid, through this story where you narrate the failed attempt of your dad to get reunited with you and your family, you reveal an understanding that goes well beyond your 5.4 years old. In the beginning you referred to the map as a *planet,* but perhaps that's how you understand your world: a planet with lines that divide cities, states and countries. A particular area that called your attention was the line between Mexico and the United States, which you retraced in blue ink to highlight the place where you say your dad crossed the border. It is indeed admirable to see you standing self-assured in front of the class ready to explain to your classmates your feelings and ideas so eloquently.

What activities could we plan to support you in exploring this topic that you are so interested in?

Zahid, we could invite you to share with your classmates the tale of your dad's travels and invite your friends to share the stories of their families too.
We could take dictations of what it means for you to be waiting for dad on this side of the border. We could support you to put into practice your interest in writing so that you could write a letter or message to your dad.
Perhaps, you would be interested in making a painting on a canvas representing your ideas and feelings with paint strokes and acrylic colors.

What's the family's perspective?

Zahid is not very fond of writing, but he talks a lot and also understands quite a lot. He doesn't like drawing but maybe with your support here at school he could find enjoyment in drawing or painting.

Mom

Learning Story 4.7 *Waiting for Dad on this side of the border*

Author: Isauro M. Escamilla

Under the same Sun

Isauro M. Escamilla

What happened? What's the story?
Zahid, of the several options we proposed to you to continue exploring the topic of the journey of your dad from Mexico to the United States, you chose a canvas, skinny paint brushes, and acrylic colors to represent the word *frontera*. Until now you had hardly showed interest in using painting tools, the process of writing or making graphic representations of your ideas. Your preferred mode of expression was to communicate orally and you have been doing it quite well! The fact you chose paint brushes and acrylic paints reveals that every child should have *the right to be an active participant* when it comes to making decisions about his or her individual learning.

What is the significance of this story?
Zahid, I'm very pleased to see your *determination* to make a graphic representation of the word *frontera* . After so many sessions singing the initial sounds corresponding to each letter of the alphabet in Spanish, I thought you would be inclined to sound out the word *frontera* phoneme by phoneme and spell it out to write it on paper, but that was not to the case. Instead, you decided to undertake something more complex and you chose a paintbrush and acrylic colors to represent (write) *frontera* the way you perceive it based on the experiences you have lived with your family and especially, with your dad.

What possibilities do emerge?
Zahid, you could perhaps share with your classmates and your family *your creative process*. Throughout the entire process of sketching and painting you demonstrated remarkable patience, since you had to wait at least 24 hours for the first layer of paint to dry before applying the next one.

You chose the color brown to paint the wall that divides Mexico and the United States because that's what you saw in the photos that popped out in the computer screen when we looked for images of the word *frontera*. You insisted on painting a yellow sun on this side of the wall because according to you, that's what your dad would see on his arrival to California, along with colorful very tall buildings with multiple windows. I hope one day you and your dad can play together under the same sun.

What's the family's perspective?
I think it is good for my son to have support from his teachers at school and that he can express what he feels or thinks.

Although sometimes I wonder if it's better to avoid the topic altogether. These months have been very difficult for everyone inthe family, but especially for him because he is the eldest. He says that he misses his dad, even though he hasn't seen him in a long time. And he says that he wants to go to Mexico when he's older to be with dad.

Learning Story 4.8 *Under the same sun*

Author: Isauro M. Escamilla

Zahid, of several options we proposed to you to continue exploring the topic of the journey of your dad from Mexico to the United States, you chose a canvas, skinny paint brushes, and acrylic colours to represent the word *frontera*. Until now you had hardly showed interest in using painting tools, the process of writing or making graphic representations of your ideas. Your preferred mode of expression was to communicate orally and you have been doing it quite well!

Further thinking

Consider the early years or school curriculum with which you are most familiar.

1. What are the powerful frameworks (the Big Ideas that provide a framing for assessment in this curriculum)? What are your favourites? Why?
2. What are some of the 'pieces' that contribute to these powerful frameworks? Can you describe the links in practice?
3. What are the key features of a 'learner self'?
4. Almost all Learning Stories will construct a learner self. Find and discuss other examples in this book.

Further reading

Carr, Margaret and Lee, Wendy (2012) *Learning Stories: Constructing Learner Identities in Early Education*. London: SAGE. Chapter 5: Recognising and re-cognising learning continuities.

New Zealand Ministry of Education (2004) *Kei tua o te Pae* Book 7 – *Assessment and Learning: Continuity*. Downloadable at: www.education.govt.nz/assets/Documents/Early-Childhood/Kei-Tua-o-te-Pae/ECEBooklet7Full.pdf (accessed 3 December 2018).

Aroha nui = With deep affection – often used in signing off letters and Learning Stories.

Paki Ako = One 'kaupapa Māori' adaptation of a Learning Story as developed by Te Kōhanga Reo o Mana Tamariki

Mauri = Vital essence, life principle, essential quality

Aroha = Love, compassion, empathy, sorrow

Kaitiaki = Trustee, custodian, guardian, protector

Papatūānuku = Earth, Earth mother

Ka pai = Well done

5

Managing Ambiguity

Writing about a research project with teachers on formative assessment and science education in schools, Beverley Bell and Bronwen Cowie wrote as follows:

> As the formative assessment done by the teachers was often unplanned and responsive, it involved uncertainties and taking risks. Formative assessment involved the teacher finding out and responding to the diverse views of students; it had indeterminate outcomes; it could not be planned in detail before the lesson; the effects of the required actions were not usually known beforehand; and usually it required the teacher to take action in the busy-ness of the classroom. Their confidence in their professional knowledge and skills was seen by the teachers to influence the degree of risk and uncertainty taken. (Beverley Bell and Bronwen Cowie, 2001: 65)

Key messages

- Uncertainty and ambiguity invite a focus on process and problem-solving
- Ambiguity and uncertainty invite collaboration and conversation
- Learning Stories encourage good thinking

Teacher question: Is it OK to be uncertain about what learning is going on?

We suggest that uncertainly is inevitable, and that managing ambiguity and uncertainty has two positive consequences, for both children and teachers: provoking *possibility thinking* and *inviting collaboration and conversation*. This is true for children, and for teachers as well.

Uncertainty and ambiguity provoke possibility thinking

Helen Haste, a writer who was part of an OECD brainstorming seminar to develop key competencies that would be needed in the twenty-first century, presents five key competencies in a book chapter entitled 'Good thinking: the creative and competent mind'. One of her key competencies has the title *Managing ambiguity and diversity*. The challenge of managing ambiguity, she says, is about the way we think.

> If children are reared to seek the single right answer and to avoid the messy and the ambiguous, they will become uneasy when confronted with multiple options and solutions. The pursuit of closure and a deep discomfort with the relativist or pluralist are the likely outcomes of exposure to such a cultural message. (Haste, 2008: 98)

We value the following comment from Debbie Meier, the principal and founder of the Central Park East School in East Harlem, writer of the books *The Power of Their Ideas* (1995) and *In Schools We Trust: Creating Communities of Learning in an Era of Testing and Standardisation* (2002). In the second of these two books she says:

> I like the fact that we are by nature unique, unpredictable, complex, never fully knowable, and endlessly varied. I'm glad that the real world doesn't come with built-in multiple-choice boxes, precoded and ready to score. ... The thing that keeps me going, on even the gloomiest days, is that element of potential surprise. (Meier, 2002: 181)

Possibility thinking

In order to make the case for teachers taking a positive view of being uncertain, we have transferred Anna Craft's four key features of creative digital engagement to describe parallel key features for creativity as a response to uncertain or ambiguous events in education environments (Craft, 2013). Her paper's title is 'Childhood, possibility thinking and wise, humanising educational futures'. It recommends harnessing playful, plural, participative creativity. Classroom studies of possibility thinking in children by Craft and her colleagues reveals that the core features of possibility thinking in children aged from 3 to 18 include the following: question posing and responding, self-determination and intentional action, being imaginative ('as if' thinking), play/playfulness (improvising), immersion (concentration), innovation and risk-taking. Possibility thinking involves finding and honing problems.

A tree, some apples and a dog

Learning Story 5.1, 'A tree, some apples and a dog', is an example of possibility thinking by a very young child. Will (the child) has only been attending this centre for a few weeks. He loves the little toy animals, and often keeps a few of them with him when he plays. His favourite is a 'little dog'. In a policy that represents this flexible setting, he was allowed to take the small animals with him when he shifted from one play area to another. On this occasion he was deeply engaged in a difficult project that he had set for himself at the light table: hanging translucent apples onto a tree on the table. Every now and then one of the apples would fall back onto the light table, so he made many mistakes although he did manage to get some of the apples to stay on the tree. Then one of them fell to the back of the light table, beyond his reach. A problem. What to do? With great ingenuity he took the little dog figure and reached over to 'hook its nose onto the troublesome apple'. The teacher was watching, but did not intervene to help. The Learning Story describes his 'sophisticated thinking' and 'strong resolve' and looks forward to noting his 'ingenuity and creativity' in other challenges.

A focus on process and problem-solving

Elliot Eisner, who was an artist as well as a creative educator, has argued for school teachers to focus on the process rather than just the product in children's play. He asks the following question in his book *Reimagining Schools*.

> Are parents helped to understand what their child has accomplished in class? ...
>
> We take the best work, and we display it. What we need to create is an educationally interpretive exhibition that explains to viewers what problems the youngsters were addressing and how they resolved them. ... I am talking about getting people to focus not so much on what the grade is, but on what process led to the outcome. (Eisner, 2005: 190)

A Tree, Some Apples and a Dog…

Will's story

Will discovered the clear apples at the light table and settled himself to hang them on the tree branches. He had to think carefully about how to do this because some of the branches on the tree have little hooks that actually become obstacles. It takes the right angle of approach and a lot of patience and coordination to get them to hang successfully.

Will managed to get quite a few apples to stay on the tree, but every now and then one would fall onto the light table. As I watched him work, one apple fell to the back of the light table – just beyond his reach.

Even though Will has only been coming to play and learn with us for a few weeks, one of the things we know about him is his absolute love for our little toy animals, and that he often has one or two with him as he plays. When the apple fell beyond his reach, Will took the little dog that was his favourite on this particular day, and used it to reach over and hook its nose onto the troublesome apple. After a couple of attempts and some impressive stretching Will had managed (with the help of the little dog) to drag the apple close enough to retrieve it and hang it onto the tree.

Will's learning

I think this is a great story for Will about his coordination and physical skills. But it is an even greater story about his persistence, and the confidence he has in his own abilities to consider challenges before him and plan with creativity the way forward to solve complex problems. This takes sophisticated thinking, an anticipation of what might happen, and a strong resolve to reach his goals.

What a great approach to learning! I am so looking forward to seeing Will take on other challenges in his play and learning, because with such a capacity for ingenuity and creativity I know without a doubt that we will all learn a lot with him and from him.

Documented with love and care for Will by Karen

Learning Story 5.1 *A tree, some apples and a dog*

Author: Karen Winderlich

Learning Stories provide one response to Eisner's question; they usually focus on the development of learning dispositions to describe the *process* of learning (children being ready and willing, as well as being able and skilful). Often, in schools, they include a commentary on both the process *and* the product, as we see with the split-screen analyses referred to in Chapter 6 and exemplified in *Learning Stories: Constructing Learner Identities in Early Education* (Carr and Lee, 2012: 17, 27, 43). In the same book, an example of combining learning episodes as product and process is also seen in the analysis of Kayla's story (Carr and Lee, 2012: 122–125). Kayla's *product* story includes language development (enunciation and articulation), art work (drawing, mask-making, patterning), literacy (using a book for reference, writing the letters of the alphabet and writing her name). Her *process* story includes a growing capacity for collaboration, exploration and the enjoyment of music and rhythm. We comment that 'It is difficult to disentangle these chains, and it is just this tangle that, over time, describes her growing identity' (Carr and Lee, 2012: 126).

Poet loves paint

Learning Story 5.2, 'Poet loves paint', is about Poet enjoying the qualities of paint. There is no product here, but the teacher recognises that this is worthy of noticing, recognising, recording and (for Poet) revisiting the experience. The Learning Story notes: 'Each time she revisits this experience Poet experiments in different ways: sometimes using the paper; sometimes a little with a brush; and sometimes all of her clothes get painted!!' The process of what paint can do (dipping, rubbing and smoothing) is emphasised. 'Where might this lead?' the Learning Story asks. The teacher makes a suggestion.

Brooke has a plan

In early childhood centres where a range of resources that have open-ended possibilities are readily available, the children are entitled and expected to use those resources in imaginative and creative ways that have meaning for them: confirming the educational implications of affective neuroscience. Sometimes they will ask for assistance, as in the Learning Story 5.3 'Brooke has a plan', which illustrates that these invitations can sometimes test a teacher's tolerance for ambiguity and uncertainty. This is an example of a teacher assisting a child to manage the process in a self-chosen task with an ambiguous and uncertain product.

The teacher is not fazed by Brooke's ambiguous and surprising plan to 'make a garden for fairies'; the story is, after all, about the process rather than the outcome. The task involved cutting fabric and using a sewing machine. She reminds Brooke that this event includes a readiness to tackle a 'tricky' task (using the sewing machine), and adds a reminder of how in the past, Brooke had tackled 'trickier and trickier' moves on the monkey bars, persevering 'day after day'. So a continuity of perseverance with difficult tasks, is established. The teacher reminds Brooke (and the family) that this task was about courage and creativity, and that these are transferable qualities. In other words, they are valuable learning dispositions.

Melissa

Poet Loves PAINT

Delicately dipping her hands into the paint on the table, Poet begins her exploration. The brush has already been discarded, that's not how Poet rolls! Instead she begins to rub the paint around on her hands and when she has a good covering there she invites the paint to move further and further up her arms. Poet's cheeks are the next to join in this experience, and this is how she spends the next 20 minutes. Dipping, rubbing and smoothing the cool paint all over skin.

What learning is happening here for Poet?

This experience is one that Bridget wrote about when Poet had only just started with us last year. I imagine that Poet must find these moments very soothing and relaxing, just as wallowing in cool mud feels on the skin. Each time she revisits this experience Poet experiments in different ways: sometimes using the paper; sometimes a little with a brush; and sometimes all of her clothes get painted!! **Where might this lead?** Whatever her research, Poet continues to enjoy the feel of paint on her skin and I wonder if she might enjoy painting in front of the mirror? We will have to invite her and see what happens.

Learning Story 5.2 *Poet loves paint*

Author: Melissa Osmond

Brooke has a plan, an imaginative one! And it requires sewing!

Brooke, today you asked me for some help. Only a little needed as it turned out! You explained what you had in mind – A garden for fairies. Yes, that would be interesting to see in 3D – from concept inside your head to fully completed art work!

My thoughts on your learning

The sewing was so very interesting because putting your fingers near a moving needle on the machine takes some courage. You made all the decisions about what you wanted, what pieces of material you required and how they would be positioned and as you progressed, you arranged these on the floor to get the best impression of the end product. You we're a little hesitant at first, but you know after all this time, that it is practice that makes the difference, and with the minimum of assistance you were there!

Where does all this creative energy lead?
Brooke you are the decision maker here and this is just one story in a very long line of creative endeavours, which you choose to involve yourself in each day. Over time your courage to pursue your goals has increased, and although this time it was using a sewing machine, it reminds me of the way day after day, you tackled trickier and trickier moves on the monkey bars. Courage is transferrable, just like creativity, and so we will be ready to write more and track your progress into the future!
Arohanui Lorraine

Learning Story 5.3 *Brooke has a plan, an imaginative one! And it requires sewing!*
Author: Lorraine Sands

Ambiguity and uncertainty invite collaboration and conversation

In assessment and assessing, ambiguity and uncertainty applies to both teachers and learners. A researcher and writer on the role of dispositions in mathematics teaching and learning, Melissa Gresalfi (2009: 362), concluded that:

> Although successful collaboration is just one of many aspects of a disposition toward engaging mathematics, it is important. Research on collaboration has documented that working with other students can create opportunities for students to engage more deeply with mathematical content than they might have done on their own. ... Specifically, groups in which students ask for help, challenge one another, and provide support create opportunities for all students to engage more deeply with content.

Gresalfi's research indicated that both successful and initially uncertain students developed dispositions towards engaging with mathematics if they were expected, entitled and obligated to participate and collaborate in the classroom. Resources in a classroom or an early childhood centre have the potential to combine the collaborative with the creative when they offer open-ended materials that provide a range of options (an 'ambiguous' agenda) for work and play. Sand, water, blocks, art materials, fabrics and so on, all encourage creativity. The value of these opportunities is highlighted in the philosophy of Reggio Emilia. In a speech in 1963, Loris Malaguzzi stated:

> Returning to the subject of our interest, we can say the more children participate really and congenially in common life, the more the need for sociality and unity is satisfied. The school group's artificial character disappears as soon as a class ceases to be a constricting environment and becomes a real life environment where children can satisfy their pleasure in growing with others. (Cagliari et al., 2016: 79)

The builders

Learning Story 5.4, 'The builders', describes two children's collaborative building in a newly established area in the centre. The area includes open-ended blocks, and in an accompanying message to the families, the teacher recognises the children's work as exemplifying the creative and collaborative work that this new building area affords:

> This is just what we hoped would happen. By paring back the resources in the construction area, James and Joshy were inspired to be creative, reflective in what they were making, thoughtful in their theorising together, and excited by seeing their work form on the floor.

The builders

James and Joshy, I was so happy to see you so engaged in building today. You worked really well together, sharing ideas on what to build and how to make your tunnels. We had planned to set up a building area to inspire children and you guys really went for it!!
I suggested you planned your building by drawing it first. You both drew some cool plans and then built what you had done. I straight away laminated them for you for our wall.

James you drew the most amazing tunnel and then made it over the picture – it was exactly the same!
You both took pride in seeing your work on the wall.
I talked about how we can leave the building out and we didn't have to break it. Joshy, you went and drew a cross and said, 'This means don't break it'. I suggested we paint it red, which you did. James, you then came up with a great idea – you painted a green cross and told me this meant that children CAN build 'next to mine'.
I waited till they were dry and I laminated them too so you can use them when you are building.
I loved seeing you draw your ideas; build them with the blocks and how excited you were to see your work on the wall. At the end of the day you shared your work with your mums – they were very impressed too!

Look at the tunnel you created. Joshy, you sat back and drew the construction; you called it a spooky Christchurch building.

Learning Story 5.4 *The builders (part 1)*
Author: Deborah Frances Rose

Dear Family,

We have some plans for building happening in the next few weeks – a new carpentry shelf unit is being built for us by the New Brighton Men's Shed and we are planning on making a building frame alongside our children to use outside. So we planned for creating a bare building area with paper, pencils and rulers to capture children's interest in planning and construction and inspire them to get creative. I was so pleased to see that on Monday morning James and Joshy were immediately inspired by this and were totally engaged in creating a very impressive structure together. I love the photo of them working side by side as this captures exactly how they were co-constructing together.

They had already started the building when I arrived at work so I introduced the idea of drawing their ideas first then building their plan. Joshy drew what they had already made and then started a drawing of a spooky Christchurch rebuild – a testament to the life of a child in a city being rebuilt around them. James drew a tunnel and then made the exact replica. I laminated them and printed a picture of the boys at work and put these straight up on the wall. The boys were so happy to see their work displayed, taking ownership of their designs and celebrating their success together.

I said we could leave the building up until after karakia and kai. Joshy went and drew a cross, 'This means you can't break it'. I said we could paint it red so the other children realise not to break it. James then had the great idea to paint a green cross. He told me that it meant 'you can build next to me'. We have added them to the building area for children to use.

This is just what we hoped would happen. By paring back the resources in the construction area, James and Joshy were inspired to be creative, reflective in what they were making, thoughtful in their theorising together and excited by seeing their work form on the floor. As I write this I can hear them building again – and Joshy asking for his work to be laminated. It is so cool to hear the excitement of their ideas in action. (Joshy is currently planning on how to build a police station and working out how to get the blocks to balance.)

Through sharing ideas and conversations about what they want to build James and Joshy are being inspired by each other, they are using resources like making the crosses to enhance their play and are being thoughtful about what to build next. And even better, their creativity is bringing other children into the construction area too. Joshy and James use a range of strategies and skills to play together including problem solving how to get their structures to stay standing as they get building. I am looking forward to seeing what they do next in this area.

Written by
Debs

Learning Story 5.4　*The builders (part 2)*

Author: Deborah Frances Rose

Teacher talk, conversation partners and ambiguity

In a very early study, Carol Feldman and James Wertsch investigated characteristics of teacher talk (Feldman and Wertsch, 1976). They were interested in and looked for markers of 'being uncertain' in teachers' speech. Twenty teachers (five from each of kindergarten, first, fourth and fifth grades) from predominantly middle-class suburban school districts served as subjects. All teachers were female and had at least one year of teaching experience. Conversations with other teachers were compared with conversations during classroom interactions. What did they find? They counted certain words as markers of uncertainty (e.g. might, maybe) against words that are markers of certainty (e.g. will, should) and found that uncertainty or doubt in teacher talk to other teachers far outweighed uncertainty or doubt in teacher talk to students. They conclude that:

> The role of teacher in an elementary school classroom seldom calls for expressions of uncertainty. The teacher is expected to be the one who knows facts, methods, and so forth, and this role expectation may limit the use of parentheticals [qualifying a statement] and uncertainty markers. (Feldman and Wertsch, 1976: 239)

That research was a long time ago; perhaps teacher talk is different now? Teachers can model being uncertain; they can also encourage children to tackle uncertain enterprises with courage.

Teachers have conversations about their Learning Stories

It is critical that teachers in any one early childhood setting get together to share the Learning Stories that they have recently written or are planning to write. They might have *noticed* an event, *recognised* it as possibly significant, and perhaps begun to *record* it in some way – with photographs or notes. There will be some uncertainty at each of these stages, and, as Melissa Gresalfi found with students and mathematical problems, conversations with others can assist with the thinking and exploration of alternative perspectives.

If teachers can seize, or create, opportunities to research their assessment practices, this is a bonus. The New Zealand Ministry of Education has provided just such opportunities. Their TLRI (Teaching and Learning Research Initiative) has included primary and early childhood teachers, together with academics. Centres of Innovation projects were initiated by teachers, who invited researchers to support their chosen topic. They were required to publish their findings, and five books of papers written by the project teams, and edited by Anne Meade, were published from these mostly three-year projects.[1]

Conversations about uncertainty

Mastering the monkey bars

Learning Story 5.5, 'Mastering the monkey bars', is about the teacher introducing uncertainty: in effect, she is constructing a 'What next?', and analysing it. She is making a resource more uncertain for the child, Samuel. He takes on a climbing track that he knows he can easily do. The teacher, who knows the child well, tells him that this activity is 'easy-peasy' – 'There is no challenge in that!' – and she moves the equipment to make his success less certain: the trail now includes the monkey bars. 'Nooo! I can't do the monkey bars!!!!' he says, and the teacher replies: 'Well, you won't do the monkey bars [an uncertain task] by walking on a plank [a certain task]; you can do it, you just have to practise'. A friend arrives and moves the equipment to make the task easier for Samuel. The teacher returns the challenge to the task. Then she stays to give him confidence, explaining that another child, Bella (who is watching), once couldn't do the monkey bars but she practised and after a while she could do it. This is a teacher who knows the children well, and is keen that just the right amount of uncertainty is a good space for learning – in this case, to call on Samuel's growing fund of courage. The successive rungs of the monkey bars enable him to self-assess his progress: building his skills until he could get to rung number four.

No more room

Learning Story 5.6, 'No more room', is about a very young child working away with a resource that has an open-ended ambiguous purpose. It is not a jigsaw, with a right or wrong solution, but it has some of the same features, and Lila may be thinking of, and trialling, the possibility of fitting them into a space. Or she may not: in this case, the objects are polished stones of irregular shape, and handling them to place them onto the tray is a sensory experience. She may be grouping them by colour? We will never know, but her focus and concentration in this self-initiated task indicates that this is a quality resource. It may well be a mathematical task too, as she fills the space, just as *Huddy hammering* in Learning Story 2.9, was covering a space with unusual materials.

Learning Stories encourage good thinking

In a chapter entitled 'Good Thinking', Helen Haste argues that:

> It has become increasingly apparent that the traditional problem-solving model, which seeks a single take on the multiple perspectives that we face in contemporary society, does not work. We must instead find ways of dealing constructively with *irreconcilable* multiple perspectives. (2008: 97)

Mastering the Monkey Bars

Dear Samuel, today I saw you at the monkey bars. There was a box and a plank under the monkey bars and that meant that you could walk across the plank without having to hold your body up with your arms – easy peasy! "Oh Samuel! There is no challenge in that!" I said and moved the plank and box away to your cries of "Noooo! I can't do the monkey bars!!!!" I said, "Well you won't learn how to do the monkey bars by walking on a plank, you can do it, you just have to practise". Next minute when I looked back I saw that your friend Bradley had moved the blue barrel under the monkey bars for you – same deal, no challenge – so meany old me shoved that away as well! This time though I stayed and encouraged you to have a go. Bella was there too and I told you that once Bella couldn't do the monkey bars but she practised and after a while she could do it – in fact she is such an expert at the monkey bars that she really makes it look effortless!

What did I learning about you today Samuel?

You took up the challenge! I was SO impressed with your courage and determination! When you first started you could just hold on to one bar, then your were able to make it to bar number two, then three, then four and then bar number five!!!! WOW!!! What an excellent effort! You went from thinking you could not do the monkey bars to trying, and building your skills till you could get to rung number five! With each new level your reached we all cheered! Bravo Samuel! I know if you keep up this awesome practice you will be able to go right across the monkey bars – you are nearly there! It's AMAZING how we can think we can't do something, but when we give it a go and don't give up we can do it – such an important lesson for life Samuel!

Written by
Arohanui, Julie

Learning Story 5.5 *Mastering the monkey bars*

Author: Julie Killick

No More Room

Lila I watched as you worked with our basket of stones today, and wanted to write this story for you because I think it shows how you are developing ever more sophisticated mathematical understandings about your world. You chose a piece of card with a picture of the stones set out in a pattern, and set about matching the stones up to the picture. You carefully laid them out around the edge of the card, and then with an equal amount of care filled in the space in between with your selection of stones.

When you were finished and the whole card was full you looked up and said. 'Look – no more room'. And of course, you were right – not even the smallest stone would fit.

What is Lila learning about?
Numeracy is woven into so much of our everyday experience. It plays a significant part of living in our world, and the best way to grow competent and confident in using it to make sense of the world is through playing around with everyday resources and objects. Using multiple objects – like Lila with the stones – gives the opportunity to work with number as well as concepts around area and space. And it is always exciting to see children playing with patterning because this builds the foundation for not only growing an understanding about numeracy, but also about literacy.

Lila you showed me today how you see the possibilities for exploring your mathematical thinking in the resources around you. You also showed how you have the cognitive skills and concentration needed to not only develop a plan but to keep it in mind until you have reached your goal.

What a great set of skills you have as a learner! I am sure I will see them in action in many more interesting experiences, and to support this to happen, I will ensure that our environment offers plenty of materials that are not only open-ended, but that are intriguing in their possibilities.

Documented with love and care for Lila by Karen

Learning Story 5.6 *No more room*

Author: Karen Winderlich

She adds, on the same page, that 'Part of this is about taking the future seriously; in all aspects of education, it is the future to which we must direct our sights'. This is an argument that threads its way through this Learning Story book; it is at the core of what we mean when we argue for *formative and fair* assessments that also recognise *powerful narratives*. Helen Haste outlines three 'challenges to the cultural framework within which education takes place' (2008: 102–104). They are shortened here:

Challenge (1) We must explore the domains of anxiety which we currently, unwittingly or otherwise, foster in young people. These include fear of open-ended or multiple solutions, fear that there may not be a reassuring single "right" answer, but several possible options.

Challenge (2) We must find ways to help young people use dialogue as a means of understanding multiple perspectives and positions.

Challenge (3) We must find a way to encourage a view of rationality that does not restrict students' resources for knowing to too narrow a cognitive perspective.

Learning Stories illustrate these as teachers notice, recognise and record Learning Stories, deal with multiple perspectives, and create opportunities for later revisiting and reflecting with the children.

Challenge (1) Explore the domains of anxiety that we might unwittingly foster

Being proud of one's work

In Learning Story 5.7, 'Being proud of one's work', the early childhood centre introduced an unfamiliar recycled pallet to the construction area. James spent some time combining the opportunities he saw in the pallet with a series of bamboo curves and blocks from the shelf, and a light rope. The teacher comments: 'I like this notion of using the unfamiliar and bringing such items into spaces offering a provocation. The intention of a provocation is to provide an invitation for a child to explore and express themselves'. These resources provided the opportunity for open-ended and multiple options, and the teacher recognised, from his stance and his smile, that he had completed a project to his satisfaction. The Learning Story *describes* his work; an *analysis* recognises the opportunities that the addition of another open-ended resource in the block area provoked, and notes the hard work and great 'work ethic'; then the *formative* part of the Learning Story invites James to assist the teacher to think about some more open-ended ('loose part' materials) that could be introduced to the block area (perhaps for his further exploration of open-ended and multiple building agendas).

Being Proud of One's Work

James spent some time in the block area today working on a large scale construction. A recycled pallet offered a different base frame to work with and build from. I like this notion of using the unfamiliar and bringing such items into spaces offering a provocation. The intention of a provocation is to provide an invitation for a child to explore and express themselves.

Selecting a series of bamboo curves from the shelf James added these, weaving the rope light through the building work.

Every so often James stopped to survey the work with his hands on hips. This stance seemed to convey a message to those around – that he was proud of the work that he was undertaking.

James spent some time on the construction and when he was finished once again stood with hands on his hips with a satisfied and contented smile upon his face.

What learning was happening here for James?

James, I can see that you have an inner confidence that comes to the surface as you engage with the world around you. Today you seemed to be pleased with your building work – and you should be as you worked really hard, demonstrating a great work ethic and focus to the job at hand.

How might we stretch this learning further?

Watching you today James has inspired me to think about what other loose part materials we could add to this space. I wonder if you might like to help me find some materials to gather from around kindergarten to assist others in their building creations? I'm sure you will have some good ideas.

Written by Kaiako Fran

Learning Story 5.7 *Being proud of one's work*

Author: Fran Paniora

Challenge (2) Find ways to help young people to use dialogue as a means of understanding multiple perspectives

Real and pretend maps

Learning Story 5.8, 'Real and pretend maps', illuminates how a map might well be seen as a metaphor for multiple perspectives and positions. Arthur has drawn a pirate map, where X marks the spot (of the treasure). Back at home, his grand-father introduces him to a real maritime map, and Arthur and the grandfather together draw a treasure map including landmarks, animals and cars; there is much discussion of maps and treasure and landmarks along the way. The photo-graphing of the story begins at home and continues at the early childhood centre, an example of learning that crosses boundaries between centre and home. Back at the centre, where the resources there provide opportunities for new perspec-tives, Arthur's imaginative pirate adventures continue: he paints a pirate flag, prepares a dinner of maggot cream pie and meat balls for the crew of the ship, and builds a telescope. The latter, too, will perhaps provide new perspectives.

Shared interests across different languages

Learning Story 5.9, 'Shared interests across different languages', illustrates how children and teachers in a multilingual environment have a unique opportunity to use dialogue as a means of understanding multiple perspectives and positions. This story follows a story written eleven days earlier, in which the teacher writes:

> Elisa, this morning you joined us for a Forest Kindergarten session. ... I noticed you and Gabriel, you picked up the magnifying glasses and walked into the wooded area: 'We're going into the forest', you said, as you held the glass close to your face.

This Learning Story continues to document this relationship. Elisa's first language is German, and Gabriel's first language is Spanish. However, the resources (magnifying glasses, books, bikes and ukulele, together with other opportunities in this Forest Kindergarten's physical environment) help the two children to construct an 'action-dialogue' that enables multiple perspectives and positions. Having different first languages was no barrier to friendship.

Challenge (3) Encourage opportunities that widen children's ways of knowing and thinking

Logical and creative thinking!

Learning Story 5.10, 'Logical and creative thinking!', is about the resources in the early childhood centre that are enabling Eden to grow a range of the characteristics

"I'm good at pretend maps but not real ones". Grandpa to the rescue! Both you and Grandpa had the Tauranga Moana map on the table and we were all looking at the real view in front of us. We checked the compass reading on your Grandpa's phone, and there we were making sure we could recognise the landmarks and seascapes, both on the map and 'for real'. Lots of discussion and decision making later you were ready to start drawing from the view in front of you. You said that trees were a tricky thing to draw and so together you and Grandpa figured this out.
My thoughts on your learning...
It was team work in action! Everyone was interested and Great Nana Doris came over to inspect your work! She gave you the seal of approval. "You're clever", she said. But you know that it is really all the practice you put in, plus your willingness to give new things a go and not give up when they are hard or tricky!!

real & pretend maps

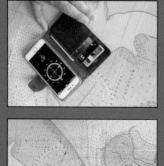

How might we stretch this learning further?
Arthur your fascination with all things 'pirates' has led you down many paths and I will add another page of photos to track some of this learning as well. We've seen your ship building and pirate cooking with your 'crew' in action in previous stories. Just now you are very interested in comparing the 'pretend maps' you draw and some real treasure maps that can lead treasure hunters to treasure by following the map! It was very useful to have your Dad's maritime map that just happened to show the harbour from our window, and together with Grandpa you drew a treasure map with all the landmarks and animals and cars in front of you. The next day at your Centre you were again drawing maps, making pirate food, reading the pirate dinosaur books and so much more I'm not fully aware of because your day is so immersed in your own plans. So this will continue because you are so passionate, and you will get better and better at looking and imagining, thinking and drawing, maps 'for real and for pretend' as a result!

Learning Story 5.8 *Real and pretend maps (part 1)*

Learning Story 5.8 *Real and pretend maps (part 2)*

Author: Lorraine Sands

Shared interests across different languages

February 4th: Elisa, this morning you joined us for a Forest Kindergarten session. After we sang our together song, it was time to explore. I noticed you and Gabriel, you picked up the magnifying glasses and walked into the wooded area, "We're going into the forest", you said, as you held the glass close to your face. You and Gabriel spent the whole session together, you seemed very busy and content with each other's company. It was really nice to observe you both making a connection in the outdoor environment. Hopefully you will both join us again next week, It will be interesting to see if this relationship develops.

February 15th: Elisa, not long after you arrived at Cowgate today, you and Gabriel found each other and from that moment on, you spent all day together. Just as you did at Forest school, you must have made a special bond and it was so lovely to witness. Gabriel's first language is Spanish and your first language is German, so you do have a shared interest in languages. You both seem to be in tune with one another, as there isn't always dialect between you, sometimes you seem to follow each other's lead through your actions. You both spent the morning outside, climbing and pushing trolleys into the small house, "This is our house", you told me. You both displayed your excellent bike skills and spent more than one hour travelling up the ramp and down again with great speed! It had been an extremely active day for you both and it was really lovely to notice you later on resting on the rocking chair as you sang and played the ukulele to your new friend. I look forward to watching this friendship blossom.

Learning Story 5.9 *Shared interests across different languages (part 1)*
Author: Kate Bowman

February 19th: Our session today was a very wet one! When we arrived we discussed the heavy rainfall and to be mindful of the pond, as the water level may be higher and also to take care as the surfaces may be slippery. Then you guys discovered something, we haven't noticed recently, giant puddles! Yourself, Gabriel and Adam all waded through the large puddle behind the Bothy and began to jump up and down. You then began to investigate the water and its properties further, as you climbed onto the higher grassy level and jumped into the water from a height, creating even bigger splashes, "Its splashing!", you commented. You and your friends repeated this many times, using your body to climb back onto the verge and taking turns to jump. I then noticed you and Adam jumping together, possibly experimenting with the cause and effect of you both jumping together?

February 26th: Elisa, it has been a pleasure to watch your interests and skills in the outdoor environment develop and we will continue to invite you to use the space on the days you are here. When we arrived, Adam began on the pile of uneven and wobbly rocks, you and Gabriel followed him. You used your whole body to manoeuvre your way across them, keeping your body low to the ground and using your feet and hands to test the stones, for stability. You seem to continually push your climbing capabilities and are always seeking new challenges to support your interest. Later I noticed you and Gabriel looking up into the trees, I could hear birds all around and I presumed you were bird watching. You spent a long time looking and discussing, Gabriel encouraged you to investigate further, "Go Elisa", "very careful". You went in deeper and reported back,"It's over the wall". Next time I will bring binoculars and bird books for you to use, if you are still interested.

I then observed you as you used the fire steel again, building on your achievements from last week. Today you created more sparks, not every time but more than last week and still, you did not give up. You then helped your friend Gabriel to use it, as he tried to strike the flint and steel together, you questioned, "What is he doing?". You then offered your knowledge and support and demonstrated how you know. It was so warming to see you wanting to share the skills you have learnt and to encourage others. Later, you experimented with it again. As I filmed, you realised there was something not quite right and you questioned, "What am I doing?". You lay the tool on the ground and swapped the pieces over to your other hand, enabling you to strike it more easily. I was amazed that you were able to alter this yourself, but each day you continue to amaze me. I look forward to inviting you to more outdoor experiences.

Learning Story 5.9   *Shared interests across different languages (part 2)*
Author: Kate Bowman

Logical and creative thinking!

Eden, you have many talents, some of these are about your characteristics as a learner and some are about being a mathematician, reader, writer, scientist! The ones I noticed today were about the way you could see something of interest and then use the materials for your own ideas. I had rummaged through the cupboards to find some more interesting bowls, and found some glass ones with unusual shapes. These certainly sparked your interest and a little while later I returned to see you deeply engaged in making your plan a reality.

My thoughts on your learning
Eden, it seems to me that you are an independent thinker! Your cake today was very different from each of the other children and even the way you thoughtfully looked at each resource to figure out its possibilities was impressively different. Those straws were particularly interesting as they filled up with play dough. Your curiosity must have been piqued because you studied these very carefully. The photo above at the top right gives an indication about the way you were deliberate in your actions. No randomness about the design, instead you carefully positioned each of the sticks and straws. This is logic and creativity merged!

How might you stretch this further?
I noticed younger children watching you and it seemed to me that your quiet leadership style was in action. I will remember to ask you for help as younger children explore these kinds of materials. Explaining how to do something to another person really stretches your thinking!
Arohanui Lorraine

Learning Story 5.10 *Logical and creative thinking!*

Author: Lorraine Sands

of being a learner, including as a mathematician, reader, writer and scientist. Here is an example where the teacher specifically spells out the knowing that includes logic, creativity, curiosity, while developing and implementing a plan to use some new resources. Her capacity to be 'deeply engaged' and a 'quiet leadership style' integrate the emotional and social with the cognitive and thoughtful problem-solving. In the final part of the Learning Story, the teacher points out that 'explaining how to do something to another person really stretches your thinking', and the Learning Story's title for a 'What next?' section (How might you stretch this further?) reminds Eden that this is her responsibility. This is the topic of the next chapter: Sharing responsibility with the learners.

Further thinking

1. Explore Helen Haste's three challenges in your own teaching and learning context (as a teacher or as a learner in a teacher education programme).
2. What challenge seems to be best modelled in the practice you know best?
3. How can these become represented in a Learning Story portfolio?

Further reading

Haste, Helen (2008) 'Good thinking: the creative and competent mind. In Anna Craft, Howard Gardner and Guy Claxton (eds), *Creativity, Wisdom, and Trusteeship: Exploring the Role of Education*. Thousand Oaks, CA: Corwin Press, pp. 96–104.

Note

1. These were published by NZCER Press in Wellington: *Catching the Waves*, 2005; *Riding the Waves*, 2006; *Cresting the Waves*, 2007; *Generating the Waves*, 2009; *Dispersing the Waves*, 2010.

Karakia = Prayer, ritual chant, incantation

6

Sharing Responsibility with the Learners

Anna Craft writes that one of the tasks in teaching for creativity is:

> adopting an inclusive approach to pedagogy, inherent in which is passing back control to the learner and in which teachers and learners enter a co-participative process around activities and explorations, posing questions, identifying problems and issues together and debating and discussing their thinking. (Anna Craft, 2005: 45)

Key messages

- Resources inspire the taking of responsibility and inventive projects
- Opportunities allow children to become relational leaders
- Opportunities encourage children to develop stories and Learning Stories

Teacher question: Do we have to teach differently for Learning Stories?

We met Helen Haste in Chapter 5 when she wrote that the first of her key (dispositional) competencies is *Managing ambiguity and diversity*. Her second is *Embracing agency and responsibility*. She comments:

> This competence refers to the ability to see oneself as an active agent in one's cognitive, social, and moral world and to take the responsibilities that go with that agency. … Research from developmental psychology indicates that this comes from having early experience taking responsibility and being effective, and being in an environment in which there is routine expectation that one will be effective. (Haste, 2008: 99)

In Chapter 3 of *Learning Stories: Constructing Learner Identities in Early Education*, 'Agency and dialogue' (Carr and Lee, 2012: 41–61), we included a quote from James Greeno and Melissa Gresalfi. That quote includes the perception that as children begin to construct themselves as learners and leaders (their identity formation) in a range of ways, there is a balance between the child's developing dispositions and the opportunities in the early childhood setting.

> Identity formation, as we understand it, is a two-way process between the individual and what he or she brings to an interaction and the resources and consequent opportunities of a particular activity setting. (Greeno and Gresalfi, 2008: 184)

We have also canvassed this idea in Chapter 3: Being Fair, where we emphasised the *opportunity to learn*. The title of Chapter 6 reminds us of the episode re-told in *Learning Stories: Constructing Learner Identities in Early Education* (Carr and Lee, 2012: 17), in which one of the four-year-old children spontaneously took up the centre's camera to record a cooking event. The teacher, who had been busy managing the making of pancakes with several children, commented later:

> Astonished, I realised that Nissa had gone and got the camera on her own and had begun to take photos. She zoomed the lens in and out, clicking the button, making sure that she photographed not just the people but the process as well.

Those photographs illustrating the Learning Story about this event were placed in the portfolios of all the children who had been cooking that day.

Resources inspire the taking of responsibility and inventive projects

In this chapter we provide three examples of Learning Stories in which children take responsibility to explore the affordance of resources in a particularly inventive or unusual way. This is another example of the person-plus (see p.43). A learner plus an open-ended resource can become an inventor of tasks, projects and games. These occasions of creativity are well worth documenting so that they can be revisited and reviewed by the children themselves, the teachers and the families; they emphasise to all the readers that self-directed learning is valued.

Grayson adds, divides and compares

Learning Story 6.1, 'Grayson adds, divides and compares', describes Grayson's interactions with an interesting resource: a large table full of small wooden cubes. Grayson appears to be interested in them as unit blocks for distributing equally into two buckets, which were also ready to hand. One of the teachers asks him, 'Grayson, what are you working on here?' He describes what he is doing: sharing and dumping. He takes them to the buckets one by one, then puts them back and grabs them in even groups for each hand and therefore for each bucket. This self-directed task, doubling for a purpose, continues. He decides to use the available tongs to pick the blocks up one by one, again distributing them evenly across the bucket containers. He focused intently on this task for some time, and knew exactly when it was completed.

Powered by intellectual curiosity

In Learning Story 6.2, 'Powered by intellectual curiosity', a number of pumpkins have arrived at the centre, and scales for weighing are readily available. Tahlia takes on the task of weighing them and, encouraged by the teacher, guessing which ones are heavier or lighter. She reads the numbers on the scale and begins to compare not only the pumpkins' weights, but also a number of other items, including a jar of pencils. This might be said to be a valuable source of 'written numbers for a purpose'; she discovers that the higher the numbers, the heavier the item. The unit for the numbers – ounces – describes an increasing scale for a purpose. It is clearly an interesting task for her, having the quality of affect that Immordino-Yang's research reminds us is a valuable ingredient for learning.

Grayson Adds, Divides and Compares

By Sabine Scherer

I noticed Grayson working at the sensory table. When I looked closer I was intrigued to see that he had dropped exactly three wood cubes in each bucket.

I was struck by the precision and intention Grayson demonstrated as he added one more cube to each bucket.

Sabine: Grayson, what are you working on here?

Grayson: I have four light blocks in each bucket. Now I have five. I'm gonna dump them back then get five again.

Grayson grabbed three cubes in each hand and deposited them into the buckets.

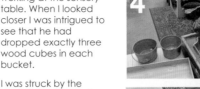
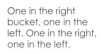

Then Grayson used the tongs to pick up individual cubes.

One in the right bucket, one in the left. One in the right, one in the left.

Grayson stopped and counted the cubes in each bucket, pointing at each cube in turn.

Grayson looked down and grabbed two fistfuls of blocks from the sensory table and dumped them into the buckets. He mixed the blocks up with his hands.

Finally, he emptied the buckets and replaced them on the table. With his pointer finger he gently touched the bottom of each bucket, and walked away.

Dear Grayson,

What did I learn about you today?

I was very interested in your work today at the sensory table with the wooden cubes. Maths was on your mind. You showed me that you have a strong understanding of numbers. You went beyond counting and one-to-one correspondence as you figured out equations in your mind. You performed addition, subtraction, even division — challenging my own schema of what maths learning can look like in a preschool classroom. This exploration and type of logical thinking came so intuitively to you.

How might we stretch this learning further?

I wonder if you have practised this skill of dividing and distributing between two on a regular basis as a result of having a sibling! Moving forward I will be looking out for the other ways that you explore these concepts and thinking of ways to support you, materials and questions to provision you with.

Love, Sabine

Learning Story 6.1 *Grayson adds, divides and compares*

Author: Sabine Scherer

Powered by Intellectual Curiosity

Dear Tahlia,

The other day I watched you use a scale to weigh a pumpkin. You said, "It's pointing to the 11". You were right, the scale was pointing to "11 ounces". I wondered what you knew about weighing things, reading scales and measuring.
I held up another larger pumpkin. "How about this one?" I asked.

You quickly said, "More".

I picked up a smaller pumpkin. "How about this one?"

"I think this one is less because it looks thinner".
You weighed the pumpkin and told me that the scale pointed to the nine. After this you proceeded to weigh everything – Adi's hat, your headband, a jar of pencils, a cup of water. After placing each item on the scale you bent down to look at the numbers.
Tahlia, it was amazing to see your learning in action. You wanted to weigh *everything*. You were excited to read the scale again and again. I am curious now to ask you, how do you think a scale works? Do you know what the numbers on the scale represent?

Teacher's reflection of the learning
Watching you reminded me of why children are the BEST learners. You make the hard work of practice and repetition look like fun and games. You are always learning, even when you are playing. Perhaps *especially* when you are playing.

Opportunities and Possibilities
Tahlia, I want to invite you back to the pumpkin weighing area tomorrow just so I can see what you will try next!

Learning Story 6.2 *Powered by intellectual curiosity*

Author: Sabine Scherer

Layers of black: the varied canvas of a busy painter

In Learning Story 6.3, 'Layers of black: the varied canvas of a busy painter', the teacher watches as Ryqal does a painting. He explores the use of layers of black and red on his canvas as well as his body. The comments by the teacher indicate (for Ryqal and his family, who will revisit this story) that she is intrigued by this experimentation. During the painting episode the teacher introduces the word 'camouflaged', which is picked up by the painting child. In the section 'My perspective of the learning here', she comments that this event has reminded her of the value of the *process*. The process on this occasion has been captured by the photographs and her commentary in the Learning Story, and she comments specifically to the family that when they retrieve the entirely black painting, they will (now) know the story behind it. She further analyses this experience in wider terms as an interest in imaginative 'transformation', linking it to Ryqal's interest in Superheroes, and she notes that the staff at the centre will notice and recognise this interest when it reappears, perhaps in another context.

Opportunities for children to become relational leaders

When young children are in a group situation, an early childhood centre or, as is the case for Learning Story 6.4, entitled 'Hold my hand', a homeless shelter, there are unique opportunities for collaborations and relationships. The key disposition here is often kindness, or empathy, as children begin to re-cognise each other and to develop relationships. We saw in the Learning Story 1.1, the boys sharing their Learning Story portfolios; this was not just about reading, it was about relationship building. Learning Story 6.4 is another example of this.

Hold my hand

We include here a Learning Story written by a teacher at Storyteller Children's Center which provides care and education for young children who are homeless, living in transitional housing or at risk for stable housing, where opportunities for the family to have agency in their lives are supported. Noelani (the child) takes on the role of a teacher, assisting another child to feel confident to climb. She is reassuring: 'I will help you, don't worry I'm here with you okay', and provides temporary support when she says, 'Hold my hand' (the name of the story). A parent response comment reveals that this written event has an on-going life: as an *imagined event*: 'As I read this I can already imagine her being so helpful to her friend' – and a *feeling*: 'It makes me feel so proud'.

LAYERS OF BLACK

THE VARIED CANVAS OF A BUSY PAINTER!   **DOCUMENTED BY HELEN**

Ryqal was painting at the easel this morning. His painting started with red, orange and blue, painted in separate but joining strokes on his paper. He stopped to ask me if I would make up some black paint. I made some black paint, handed him the pot and preceded to sit back and watch him with fascination. Ryqal began to slowly paint over his earlier colours with the black paint. Soon the entire paper was covered in black, and he took care to cover the very top and edges too.

Then leaving the paper for a while, he chose to paint his hand, using this as the canvas instead. He covered his right hand with the red paint. He said to me as he was painting: *"My hand* (showing me) *has turned this colour* (red) *because I have different hands". "The other day I painted my hand blue and I went to New World and my hand was still blue. Batman has this colour but blue eyes".*

He then transformed his hand again, this time from red to black and the painting got higher up his arms until it reached near his elbow – almost like a long glove. At one point he held his black painted arm up over the paper, black on black. I commented that his arm was now difficult to see as it was camouflaged. He looked pleased, a smile sweeping across his face.

He then set to painting his left hand and arm. *"Now my other hand is camouflaged",* he said. *"My (other) hand is dried up so I have to paint it again".* And so he continued for another 5–10 minutes, enjoying the process and the outcome. When he felt he was finished, he took himself to the bathroom and washed his hands and arms meticulously – not a drop of evidence (other than these photos) to show what he had been up to!

My perspective of the learning here
What a neat reminder of the importance and value of the *process* rather than the *product* – Ryqal reminded me of this today. I felt an initial "oh no he's going to cover his beautiful painting with black" (but I never said this). It is easy as an adult watching to place emphasis on the *product*: the painting, and yet when I watched Ryqal and his processes of transformation both on and off the paper, I was reminded about the amazing learning that happens in the *process* of painting. So Atisah and Owen, when you retrieve the black covered painting, you will now know a bit of the story behind it! ☺

Although Ryqal is relatively independent from adults in his play, he is confident to share his ideas and ask for materials (such as black paint) to extend his play ideas. And when Ryqal wants to tell you something, he does! I am enjoying more conversations like this with Ryqal and this tells us that he is feeling more comfortable and confident. He has an elaborate imagination and interest in Superheroes and their power of transformation and I wonder whether this influenced his decision in transforming his painting and parts of his body today. And of course there is the sensory pleasure in painting his hands and feeling the textures of the paint, and watching colours transform before his eyes.

We will continue to support Ryqal in his creative endeavours, including his interest in transformation. Where will you take this next I wonder Ryqal?

Links with the early childhood curriculum *Te Whāriki* (Ministry of Education 2017) Communication – Discovering different ways to be creative and expressive – expressing their feelings and ideas using a wide range of materials and modes – in this case the language of visual art
Exploration – Play is valued as meaningful learning and the importance of spontaneous play is recognised – Playing, imagining, inventing and experimenting
Contribution – Being affirmed as individuals – recognising and appreciating own ability to learn and use a range of strategies and skills to support own learning

Learning Story 6.3 *Layers of black: the varied canvas of a busy painter*
Author: Helen Aitken

Hold My Hand

Observation

Noelani, I really enjoy seeing you become a leader outdoors, enjoying the nature field trips with WYP. I noticed how you were attentive towards your peers, offering to help anytime they needed. Today you were leading your friend Kaylani to climb up the little mountain by holding her hand and saying, "I will help you, don't worry I'm here with you, okay". Then Kaylani responded, "Ok, Noelani". Next, you gave instructions on what to do. "Ok, hold my hand. I'm here with you, next to you. Ok, don't worry; you are doing a very good job climbing. "I know it is hard to climb, but just keep holding my hand and step where I stepped so you can be safe, like me". I was so amazed how you were helping your friend at all times. You were so confident making sure your friend had fun while climbing and sliding down the mountain! I also noticed how nature transforms you to think about how to take care of plants and birds as the day goes by. It is so hard for you to hear that it is lunch time, because it means that our time in nature is almost finished for the day. You show your big smile; it is contagious! Everyone smiles and feels calm, like you. I have watched you taking turns during the field trip to play with each friend. You were careful to give enough time and attention during playing time and the relationship is becoming stronger each time.

What it means

Noelani, today you were helping your friends to feel secure by encouraging them to climb up and offering to help by holding their hand. You were using your words to make your friends feel secure, and praised them a lot during your adventure. You are really good at observing and assessing the environment to plan ahead as to how safe it was. You have strong empathy and emotional readiness to assess who will need help. You offer help to others while exploring and making peers feel comfortable with body and surrounding around them.

Possibilities and opportunities

Noelani, I will provide more opportunities to you to help your peers to connect with nature. We can plan field trips to Oak Park to explore the creek and surroundings. I will provide color or oil pastels to draw pictures of our nature exploration to help your abilities of connection with Mother Earth as well your artistic creativity you have shown in class.

DRDP

ATL-REG 1 BE, 3 BE, 4 BE, 5 BE, 6 BE, 7 BE, SED 2 BE, 4 BE, LLD 3 BE, 4 BE, COG 9 BE, 10 BE, 11 BE, PD-HLTH 1 BE, 2 BE, 5 BE, 9 BE,

Parent's response

It makes me feel so proud knowing that Noelani is so caring and loving to others around her. As I read this I can already imagine her being so helpful to her friend. Everyday she amazes me with the things that she does and I feel proud of her. Noelani is a girl who loves to help others and she also loves to be outdoors.

Learning Story 6.4 *Hold my hand*

Author: Alicia Jimenez

The group leader

Learning Story 6.5, 'The group leader', is a story from a centre in China where Yici became a group leader for the day. The story notes the expected responsibilities: to organise group discussion, to manage the observation book, and to record group observation. The teacher praises her for the way she deals with the relationships with her peers, and also her attitude towards constructive feedback.

Drawing hands

Learning Story 6.6, 'Drawing hands', from China, reflects an early experience (Haohao is five and a half years old) of taking responsibility for assisting an adult artist. He always prepares brush, ink and paper for the teacher, an artist who paints and does observational drawings outdoor every day. Haohao is 'having early experience taking responsibility and being effective' (see the Helen Haste quote early in this chapter), and is in an environment in which there is routine expectation that children will be effective. He is building 'the ability to see oneself as an active agent on one's cognitive, social, and moral world and to take the responsibilities that go with that agency' as Helen Haste commented. He watches the teacher drawing, and on this occasion he imitates her process – drawing hands – and is critical of his own drawing. He says with a frown, 'What a fat hand!'. There is a suggestion for the future that he might become able to contribute to an exhibition of teachers' and children's art.

Teachers and children in primary school writing Learning Stories

In 2007, a new school curriculum was developed in New Zealand. This included not only the school subjects in some detail for each level of primary school, but also, influenced by OECD work (Rychen and Salganik, 2003), an array of five key competencies was developed: (i) Thinking, (ii) Using language, symbols and texts, (iii) Managing self, (iv) Relating to others, and (v) Participating and contributing. Some primary schools became very interested in finding ways to assess these dispositional qualities in the curriculum; looking to early childhood as a model, a number of schools began to introduce Learning Stories. In a research project, we documented and wrote up these early school assessments in response to this strong interest, developing a resource booklet that includes readings, five workshops and an accompanying DVD (Davis et al., 2013: 54; Transcript in Workshop 5).

One of the tasks for the teachers was to 'Talk about your story with another teacher':

- How did you feel about writing the Learning Story?
- Which aspect came easily?
- Sharing the story: how could this story provide useful feedback to the student and family (or the students and the families, if this is a group story)?

The Group Leader

Child: Yici Liu

Teacher: Wei Feng

It was Wednesday again, time to observe the plants. You had all votes from the group members and became the group leader for the day. You happily accepted the role. This was your third time to be the group leader, so you knew your responsibility very well, that is: to organise group discussion, to manage the observational book and record group observation.

A child pointed out a mistake you made at one stage when you recorded the observation. You took his suggestion with a smile on your face and made some revisions.

<u>What leaning is happening?</u>

It is very good to see you open to suggestions, Yici! I am amazed with not only the way you deal with the relationships with your peers but also your attitude and strategy towards constructive feedback. I have noticed you have improved a lot. I keep finding something to make you shine every time when I write Learning Stories for you.

Learning Story 6.5 *The group leader*

Author: Wei Feng

Drawing hands

Documentation by Haohao (five and half years old) and Huang (teacher)

You like listening to the stories about the Cave of 1000 Buddhas told by Teacher Maomao. A week ago, Teacher Maomao started to copy the instrument players' hands from the Cave of 1000 Buddhas. You always prepared brush, ink and paper and watched how she drew every time. You asked her a lot of questions but never tried to draw by yourself. I think you start to become interested in Chinese painting and the art work in the Cave of the 1000 Buddhas, which you have never had any chances to experience before. I can feel you like and admire Teacher Maomao

Today, when Teacher Maomao started her drawing, you sat next to her, and then you started to copy the picture from the Cave of 1000 Buddhas. You have seen the picture for many days now.

The picture you copied was a hand with a bracelet. There was a little flat thin piece for picking the strings on the instrument in the hand too. It was your first time holding a brush. Even though you tried to copy Teacher Maomao, the way you held the brush was still like how you held a crayon. You started from the bracelet, then you moved onto the fingers and the flat thin piece. You stopped and looked at the picture every time you drew a stroke. When you finished the picture, you said with a frown, "What a fat hand!"

You continued to draw the second hand. This time you drew the palm too small, so you didn't have enough space for fingers. You corrected it and started to colour your first draft.

You spent 45 minutes copying the hands. I could see you draw every single stroke with extra care. You must have taken time to think.

What did I learn about Haohao today?
Your long-time observation is actually the preparation for your new learning. You were very engaged when you drew. You observed and thought actively and persisted. You must want to become an artist like Teacher Maomao.

What next?
Teacher Maomao paints and does observational drawings outdoors every day. What happy learning time for you! She is preparing for an exhibition with teachers' and children's art work. Do you want to show your work together with hers at the exhibition?

 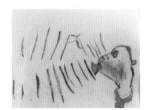

Learning Story 6.6 *Drawing hands*
Author: Huang Yuxin

- How might this story open the door for the student(s) and family/families to contribute to this assessment and to the next steps in the learning. (Davis et al., 2013: 28)

In one school, the children began to write their own Learning Stories. Here is Cameron, a student, commenting in the DVD on the process (Davis et al., 2013: 54):

> When the first time we really start writing one of these [Learning Stories] you don't really know what to do. You don't know what to say and you have to write your own little blurb at the bottom. But when you get to, like, to probably your third Learning Story it gets kind of really easy.

Opportunities for children to develop stories and Learning Stories

We introduced Vivian Gussin Paley in Chapter 3. Classic examples of children directing their own learning, and being willing – more than willing – to do so, are documented in Paley's books. Paley's pedagogy includes open-ended conversations with groups of children. She also invites children to tell imaginative stories, which she writes down. The storyteller then directs the drama as children (including the author of the story) act it. Her books have titles that immediately engage us: *White Teacher* (1979), *Wally's Stories: Conversations in the Kindergarten* (1981), *Boys and Girls: Superheroes in the Doll Corner* (1984), *Bad Guys Don't Have Birthdays* (1988), *The Boy Who Would Be a Helicopter* (1991), *Mollie Is Three* (1986), *You Can't Say You Can't Play* (1992), *The Girl with the Brown Crayon* (1997), *The Kindness of Children* (1999), *A Child's Work (The Importance of Fantasy Play)* (2004).[1]

In Chapter 4, Learning Story 4.4, a child asks how to write a Learning Story. She dictates one, and then takes photographs to accompany it.

Developing a love of literacy

Learning Story 6.7, 'Developing a love of literacy', is about Ethan telling a story. These examples of early storytelling are important to include in the children's portfolio. For many children they are their first attempt. As their attempts continue, and the storyline becomes more complex, this development will be recorded. The revisiting and reviewing will support and deepen the 'love of literacy', which is where it began. This is a story about a beloved character, T-Rex.

Finding wonderment in the rainbow fish!

Learning Story 6.8, 'Finding wonderment in the rainbow fish!', is about distributed learning. Young children will often pick up an idea introduced by a teacher, and explore it in personal ways. In this example, Bobbie-Rose picked up an image

Developing a love of literacy

Nadine

This morning Ethan, you and I spent some time together at the drawing table outside. You were drawing a picture and told me that it was a dinosaur. 'It's a T-Rex, T-Rex say "Roar!" He scary. T-Rex have sharp teeth'. I wrote your story down on a piece of paper and suggested that you could make a book about a T-Rex. You liked this idea Ethan, and saw it as a plan for your learning. You began work on the next page of your book, and thought about some of the different features of the T-Rex. You drew his eyes, his hair and his legs. The last page in your book was about the scary T-Rex eating a tree. We then talked about a title page for your book. We called your book, 'Ethan's T-Rex Book' and you once again practised your drawing.

The next job was to go to the book binder inside and bind your pages together. You pulled the handle down and this crunched the holes to create the spine. We threaded your pages on to a plastic coil, and then your book was complete!

What learning do I see happening for Ethan?

Books are a great way for young children to develop an understanding about literacy. Making books has been part of our curriculum for some time now, and today Ethan discovered this as a possibility for his own learning.

In the early years literacy learning is about meaningful and purposeful exploration of the different forms of literacy, and developing a love of reading and writing. Drawing pictures and turning them into books is a way for Ethan to develop important understandings around how to tell a story, and that his spoken words can be written down and read by others. Engaging in learning experiences such as book-making is fostering the development of Ethan's oral literacy skills, and he is becoming more and more confident in sharing his ideas and thoughts with others.

Book 17 of Kei tua o te Pae/Assessment for Learning, acknowledges the importance in the early years of establishing a sound oral foundation, particularly in the realms of conversation and storytelling. This foundation is integral to the development of reading and writing. We know that if children have a sound

knowledge and understanding of oral literacy, this will support their development of reading and writing.

One of the learning outcomes in Te Whāriki, our early childhood curriculum, is for children to enjoy hearing stories and retelling and creating them. We will continue to encourage this learning outcome for Ethan, and through this he will continue to develop his oral, written and visual literacy learning.

Learning Story 6.7 *Developing a love of literacy*

Author: Nadine Priebs

Finding Wonderment in the Rainbow

Tena Koe Bobbie-Rose, a while ago now, I read my book *The Rainbow Fish* by Marc us Pfister and offered this as inspiration for creativity at the art table. Initially, you weren't involved in this but must have been observing from a distance. I knew this, as the following day you got busy at the art table, crayon and dye were your choice of medium. Once you had finished, you brought your creation to me – "Look Heidi, it's a rainbow fish for you". After this, another rainbow fish creation followed, then another and another. I tucked these away inside my *Rainbow Fish* book, interested to see what might become of them.

Keeping these in a safe place I felt, really showed you that I valued your work and through the next few weeks I would learn that this small notion would evolve into a whole gallery of rainbow fish creations. This is how I know that you also are placing value upon your own work, realising that what you have created is something special – that what you are producing really is amazing!

Every day for the past few weeks you have taken yourself over to the art table. I have watched you carefully select what you needed before entering your creative zone. Sometimes you ask for help with the tail and we are now only drawing three dots for you to join together. Pretty soon, with a little more encouragement I know you will be completing this on your own. Sometimes you have information to share about your creations – "This one has rainbow water, then the rainbow fish will be happy" – or you will reflect upon the story and discuss how you thought the rainbow fish was kind in sharing his scales, relating it to examples of kindness within our centre. The overall message in the story has definitely captured your attention. One of your creations got you thinking about the structure of a fish – "Why do fish have tails?" you wondered. "How will we find out?" I asked. You then took it upon yourself to ask those around you. Jeena and Jayda-Maire both shared that they thought it was so that fish could swim.

What learning do I think is happening here?

Bobbie-Rose has found her drawing niche within the rainbow fish and is willing to continue exploring each avenue that this provides. I have been really thinking about what it is that is fuelling this exploration and repetition, and I feel that most of all Bobbie-Rose is drawn to the wonderment of the rainbow fish and what it represents. She is able to feel a sense of self-satisfaction through engaging in this creative process each time she enters the art area. In these moments she is sure of herself, her intentions and can find fulfilment in the end result. Over time, I feel that the rainbow fish will transcend, as Bobbie-Rose discovers even more inspiration that provokes her creative desires within.

Opportunities and possibilities?

Together Bobbie and I have discussed creating a book with all her creations. I am excited to see how this will come together and where it may lead to next.

Your mum suggested that introducing screen printing might be another way to expand your creative horizons and earlier on in the week we have been learning alongside one another through exploring and experimenting with this media (as I too am discovering the techniques and processes involved in screen printing).

Mum tells me that your passion for rainbow fish is also flowing through into your home environment. Last night you arranged all the sparkly glitter nail polishes that your Aunty Rachel had given you – in the shape of a rainbow fish.

Other special people in your family are also considering ways that they can support your passion for rainbow fish art. Lao Lao (your grandma) brought in some glitter glue pens as well as the glittery nail polish from your Aunty Rachel for you to use, which we will continue exploring this week!

Learning Story 6.8 *Finding wonderment in the rainbow fish!*

Author: Heidi Hammann

from a teacher's reading of the book *The Rainbow Fish*, not immediately, but a day later. This interest shifted place and mode, as reported by her mother. What developed from her love of this book was a 'whole gallery' of rainbow fish pictures, drawn and coloured by Bobbie-Rose using a range of media. She became curious: 'Why do fish have tails?'. The teacher asks her, 'How will we find out?' and Bobbie-Rose asked two children the question, and they supplied the answer. So this was a collaboration between Bobbie-Rose, a teacher, a book, some art materials and two other children: a good example of distributed learning.

Purerehua butterfly

Learning Story 6.9, 'Purerehua butterfly', comments that earlier stories have recorded that Jaxon is an explorer of nature and has a love of books. This story begins with Jaxon seeing a white butterfly and rushing off to consult the 'big butterfly book'. It also records a special moment at the centre: a beautiful chrysalis hanging from a pot plant. We are again reminded of David Perkins' *Making Learning Whole*, referred to earlier in this book. For Jaxon, his love of butterflies (he often puts on the butterfly cape and 'flutters about'), his sighting of a white butterfly, his interest in books and reading (especially perhaps, a big book at the centre about butterflies), and the discovery of the chrysalis, were linked together – and reified – in this Learning Story.

Further thinking

1. What resources for young children do you consider 'call' to the children. Can you write a Learning Story that reflects this?
2. In the context that you know best, what opportunities are there for children to take on leadership?
3. Consider ways in which children can be encouraged to recognise the learning goals here.
4. In what ways and on what occasions are children in early years provision and schools enabled to assess their own learning (and, perhaps, to dictate their own Learning Stories)?

Further reading

Carr, Margaret and Lee, Wendy (2012) *Learning Stories: Constructing Learner Identities in Early Education*. London: SAGE. Chapter 3: Agency and dialogue.
New Zealand Ministry of Education (2004) *Kei tua o te Pae* Book 4 – *Children Contributing to their Own Assessment*. Downloadable at: www.education. govt.nz/assets/Documents/Early-Childhood/Kei-Tua-o-te-Pae/ECEBooklet4 Full.pdf (accessed 3 December 2018).

Pūrerehua Butterfly

Whangia ka tupu, ka puāwai

That which is nurtured blossoms and grows

We know that Jaxon is curious about nature and an explorer of the natural world. In earlier stories we have shared his love of books and reading. He came to me full of excitement one day taking me by the hand and pointing at a white butterfly, he then raced off to get the big butterfly book. He pointed at the butterflies in the book then at the butterfly. As we were watching and talking about the butterfly another one came and then another, e toru nga purerehua. So beautiful to watch as they flutter about. Jaxon made the connection with the butterflies and the book. Jaxon has a growing literacy knowledge, recognising print symbols and concepts, using them with enjoyment, meaning and purpose/he kōrero pāngarau.

Jaxon often puts on the butterfly cape and flutters about. This interest was further supported to our surprise by a beautiful chrysalis hanging from a pot plant (a surprise to us all). Jaxon of course was one of the first to discover this. He spent quite some time carefully observing and using the big book again as a resource.

How might we stretch Jaxon's learning further
I have a swan plant with eggs at home and will bring this in to share with Jaxon. I also wonder if Jaxon would like to have a go at drawing as a way of expressing his interest in purerehua, kaiako will talk with Jaxon about this idea.

Nā Gae march 2018

Learning Story 6.9 *Pūrerehua butterfly*
Author: Gae Thawley

Notes

1. Published by Harvard University Press, Cambridge, MA, except for *Boys & Girls: Super-heroes in the Doll Corner* (1984), *Mollie Is Three* (1986), *Bad Guys Don't Have Birthdays* (1988), *A Child's Work: The Importance of Fantasy Play* (2004). These four were published by the University of Chicago Press, Chicago.

2. This Learning Story includes mandated developmental assessment required by the funding agency for this Head Start program.

Pūrerehua = Butterfly

Nā = From, by

7

Developing Partnerships With Families

Urie Bronfenbrenner writes about a critical element for achieving harmony in human relations:

> We must begin by engaging children and adults in common activities. Here, integration across class and culture is not enough. ... What is needed in addition is a context in which adults and children can pursue together a superordinate goal, for there is nothing so 'real and compelling to all concerned' as the need of a young child for the care and attention of his elders. The difficulty is that we have not yet provided the opportunities – the institutional setting – that would make possible the recognition and pursuit of such cross-generational experiences on a regular basis. (Urie Bronfenbrenner, 2005: 207–208)

Key messages

- Learning Stories create cross-generational conversations
- Learner identities cross boundaries
- Keep learning in the foreground: the use of both paper-based and e-portfolios
- Recognise family aspirations

Teacher question: How do we enable and encourage families to read and respond to the Learning Stories?

Learning Stories create cross-generational conversations

Many early childhood settings and schools have indeed provided an institutional setting for cross-generational experiences on a regular basis (see the Bronfenbrenner quote at the beginning of the chapter). A portfolio of Learning Stories becomes a 'boundary object' that crosses the generations. It is owned and read by the children, and read and commented on by families. Teachers sometimes write Learning Stories not just as formative assessment artefacts for the children and the other teachers, but also with an additional comment with the children's families in mind as readers and responders.

Learning Stories that both make connections with families and focus on progressing the learning

Weaving and more, French knitting, Making connections

This is a series of three Learning Stories (7.1 'Weaving and more', 7.2 'French knitting' and 7.3 'Making connections') that link together in two ways. Increasingly complex weaving/knitting enterprises, connects to the sharing of this work with a mother and then a grandmother. The teacher has introduced weaving 'to extend the interest that kindergarten tamariki (children) have in beading'. She writes this Learning Story to Violet, and reminds her that this is about 'facing a challenge'. This story is destined for home, too, and the teacher, Christine, includes a link to a video by Carol Dweck, the Professor of Psychology, discussing the value of a *growth mindset*. She includes a section on 'What next?', and suggests ways to add complexity to the weaving: trying some French knitting. This Learning Story is followed by another: Christine brings the French knitting 'loom' to the kindergarten in the morning, shares the new venture with Violet's mother, who suggests that the grandmother might become engaged; the knitting loom goes home for the weekend when Grandma comes to stay. The teacher writes in the story about her own intergenerational learning, noting that 'craft connects them (the generations)'. It is a nice version of the way a portfolio can document the developing person-plus, an idea that was introduced in Chapter 6 – and of the significant way in which craftwork and knowledge is handed down from one generation to another, and in the process, the relationship between the three generations is enriching them all. The craft did the work, and later, the portfolio will be a source of conversations about the connection at that time. In two of these Learning Stories the teacher adds a proverb in te reo Māori.

A quiet moment

Learning Story 7.4, 'A quiet moment', is about Ashlie talking with her grandfather, with her portfolio as the common focus. A portfolio is thus an *affordance* for a genuine conversation where the child is the authority: she knows the detail behind the Learning Stories, and she can add further explanation. It includes the teacher comment to Ashlie: 'your portfolio is a tool that you can use to explore, to share information, and to recall previous experiences'. Ashlie is also reminded that she can take her portfolio home any time she likes – and that the grandfather can come and visit her at kindergarten whenever he has a quiet moment.

Welcome Stories

A number of centres have begun to use the term 'Welcome Stories', which document a first day, or a first day without family, at the centre. There are a number of purposes for this. Firstly, to reassure the family about the wellbeing of the baby or the toddler or the child; secondly, to describe some of the routines in action on that day; and finally, to illustrate the Learning Story format as an assessment and the portfolio that is being created. 'Talofa Lily' is one of these Learning Stories.

Talofa Lily

Learning Story 7.5, 'Talofa Lily', has all the qualities of a Welcome Story. It describes Lily's happy day, and photographs confirm this. It also promises the family that at this centre Lily's teachers will do their best to 'read her cues' and to 'follow the routines you have already established at home'. Furthermore, on her first day at the nursery a familiar person visited and sang to her in Samoan. It is about the planning for support and care with respect to a 'powerful narrative' (see Chapter 4) – wellbeing and belonging – the relationships and routines that Lily will experience in this place. It is also the first Learning Story, and will be housed in her very own portfolio. A second Learning Story 7.6, 'O le Malaga fa'alea'oa'oga a Lily', is written firstly (part 1) in the Samoan language and then in English (part 2).

Violet

Christine.
To extend on the interest kindergarten tamariki have in beading I was interested to see what the response would be to weaving. In the past, kaiako Ariana worked some harekeke/flax with the tamariki, which would have been great, but with no time to prepare the harekeke/flax I set up some paper weaving frames and some strips of colourful paper, then I invited tamariki to give it a go.
Violet, when you settled yourself in one of your favourite areas, the art area, you came and sat close to me watching at first, I invited you to give it a go. You began with an easy openness to see what needed to be done. I explained the process, the concept and gave you some tips. To begin with we wove the paper together but I could see that you really didn't need my help, so after just a very short while I sat back and watched as you confidently wove.

My thoughts on your learning
I mentioned to your mum how impressive you were today, Violet. You captured the concept of under and over and opposite under and over on the next line so quickly. Capturing concepts so quickly shows the deeper understanding you have of how things work. Your experience with art, craft and life all come together to support you to develop new understandings. As you face any new challenges I can see you feel confident that with all your knowledge and experience you will give things a go, you have a growth mindset. Having this attitude to learning you will naturally develop and grow more concepts and understandings. Carol Dweck, a Professor of Psychology, discusses having a growth mindset in this link to a video of Carol:
www.youtube.com/watch?v=isHM1rEd3GE&t=85s I wonder if your family would like to watch it?

Where can you take your learning next?
I love to spin and knit wool and over the years I have had a lot of satisfaction at challenging myself to the complexities of these crafts. I have noticed that you also love to make things with your hands, especially with threading beads. I have seen you develop your craft of beading, adding complexity as you go, I wonder if now you wish to develop your skill of weaving paper or harekeke? Or perhaps try some French knitting. Let's get together to explore these crafts.
'Whala te iti kahuranga ki te tuahu koe me he maunga teitei'.
Aim for the highest cloud so that if you miss it, you will hit a lofty mountain.

Learning Story 7.1 *Weaving and more*
Author: Christine Bailey

French Knitting

Violet

Christine.
Violet, from your last story about weaving paper we have now also tried French knitting.
On the weekend I went to Spotlight to find some French knitters, luckily they had some there. I then found some wool and prepared a little knitting so when you arrived on Monday morning we would be ready to try it out.
Monday morning arrived and I shared what I had brought along with you and your mummy. I showed the knitting part of how to do it and together you and your mummy learned together. You worked on the process, the tension required and the best place to hold it, it is different for everyone, you just have to get the feel of it that best suits you as an individual. I could see that you captured the concept once again, like the earlier paper weaving concept, so quickly.
In the quiet part of the afternoon you came to me again and asked if you could do some more. I didn't need to hold the knitter this time, you settled yourself in a comfy place and got to work. One of the other tamariki came along, he was interested in what you were doing.
Your mum mentioned that your grandma, who does crochet, was going to visit you on the weekend so I suggested maybe you would like to take the knitter home and share your new craft with your grandma.
We would love to see some photos of this, if it happens.

Learning Story 7.2 *French knitting*
Author: Christine Bailey

Making Connections

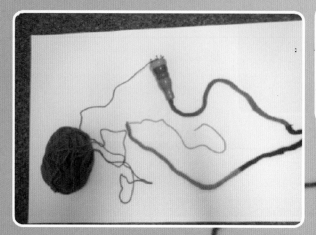

Roy Specter 1936

Gottfried Lindauer 1903

Violet
Christine
Violet, you and your grandma did indeed spend time together French knitting during the weekend she visited. You proudly showed me the results of your efforts when you returned to kindergarten the following week. I was so impressed with how much knitting you both had managed to accomplish.

My thoughts on your learning.
The shared experience of French knitting with your grandma touched my heart. For generations women have shared their craft, passing on knowledge and experience to others. My mother taught me how to knit and then she taught my daughter.
This link between generations is a prized one as craft connects them.
Crafting things takes time so women and children would gather and chat while they crafted and created. Deep discussions would ensue, people taking time to make sense of the world around them, coming up with ways to make this world a better place. In this busy world having such an opportunity is one to be treasured and revisited.

Where might you take this learning next?
Now the new year is with us I hope we can grow this knitting interest, teach others and share understandings.
Maybe we can inspire your mum to learn to knit too.

'Hapaitia te ara tika pumau ai te rangatiratanga mo nga uri whakatipu'.

Foster the pathway of knowledge to strength, independence and growth for future generations.

Learning Story 7.3 *Making connections*
Author: Christine Bailey

A Quiet moment

Kim

This morning when you came to kindergarten, Ashlee, you excitedly shared the news that your grandad, who you call Gung Gung, was going to pick you up from kindergarten this afternoon. Every now and then throughout the morning you reminded me about this and when it came to the end of the day, there was Gung Gung. He was very keen to see all that you do at kindergarten and asked to see your portfolio. Ashlee, you sat on the couch next to your Gung Gung, turning the pages and revisiting your learning with him. This was such a lovely sight to behold, a quiet moment shared with Gung Gung.

Ashlee, we know the importance of being able to revisit experiences with family and friends, and your portfolio is a tool that you can use to explore, to share information, and to recall previous experiences.

Ashlee, your Gung Gung took great delight in reading your stories and learning about what happens at kindergarten, and I could see that you were very excited to be able to share your learning with him.

Ashlee, you can take your portfolio home any time you like, and Gung Gung can come and visit you at kindergarten whenever he has a quiet moment.

Learning Story 7.4 *A quiet moment*

Author: Kim Parkinson

Talofa Lily

Talofa Lily, and a big warm welcome to you and your family/whanau. I am looking forward to getting to know you and supporting you to establish a sense of well-being and belonging in your new environment.

Lily, today was your first day in the nursery, you enjoyed playing on the floor and had a lovely big smile for everyone you met. You seem like a very relaxed and sociable wee girl. Tinâ came to visit and sang to you in Samoan, I'm sure having a familiar face and voice close by was a great comfort for you.

Mum recorded your daily routines for me and you certainly let me know when you were hungry or tired. You even settled yourself off to sleep in your new bed.

Lily, I will do my best to read your cues and to follow the routines you have already established at home. I will also ensure that these routines are carried out in a calm and respectful manner.

For you to feel safe and secure it is important that you gain trust, so my focus will be on supporting you to build trusting relationships with your teachers, your peers and your new environment.

Welcome once again Lily, Lisa and Scott. I look forward to being part of Lily's learning journey and working in partnership to ensure that your time here at Lincoln University Childcare and Preschool is happy, fun and rewarding.

Learning Story 7.5 *Talofa Lily*
Author: Julie Manson

O le malaga fa'alea'oa'oga a Lily Tasia in Lincoln Childcare & Preschool.

Kaiako: Ruta McKenzie

Ua tolu nei vaiaso talu ona amata lau malaga fa'alea'oa'oaga Lily Tasia i le A'oga Amata a Lincoln Childcare Preschool. Sa fa'aalia ou uiga fiafia ina ua lua feiloai ma lou Tinâ matua e ala i lana pese e masani ona usu pe a lua feiloa'i i le tatou aiga.

Sa e pulato'a ma fa'alogo a'o pese tina ma sa ou mautinoa ai lou fiafia ina ua e vaai iâ Tinâ.

I le vaiaso nei sa toe pese foi Tinâ i lana pese masani e fa'afeiloai ai oe ina ua ou ulufale atu i le si'osi'omaga o pepe. Na vave ona e fetilofa'i solo ina ua e fa'alogo i le leo o Tinâ ma sa fa'aalia ou foliga ataata.

I le taimi o vaiaiga o le aoauli na asiasi mai ai lou tama matua (grandpa) e vaai oe i le Aoga Amata. O uiga ataata ma le fiafia sa maitauina ina ua lua feiloai i lea taimi. Ou te talitonu sa e fiafia tele ina ua maua le lua mafutaga ma grandpa e talatalanoa ai, aemaise o lana fesoasoani mo oe i le taimi o lau taumafataga fa'apea le suiina o lou napetini.

Ia maua pea lou fiafia Lily Tasia i totonu o le siosiomaga a le Aoga Amata, ma ole a fa'auauina pea ta talanoaga I le Gagana Samoa e ala i pesepesega ma talanoaga fa'asamasamanoa.

Learning Story 7.6 *O le Malaga fa'alea'oa'oga a Lily Tasia in Lincoln Childcare and Preschool (part 1)*

Author: Ruta McKenzie

Lily Tasia's first journey to Lincoln Childcare & Preschool

Translation

This was your third week of your educational journey to Lincoln Childcare and Preschool, Lily, and you were so delighted to see your grandmother singing and to hear the welcome song that she sings to you when she comes and visits you at your home.

Singing has been a big part of your upbringing and your grandmother is continuing to sing with you when you come to the nursery.

During lunch break, your grandfather came to visit you. You were so delighted to see your grandpa, greeting him with a big smile, and he was so pleased to feed you as well.

Lily Tasia, your grandmother will continue to sing and have conversations with you in Samoan language at the childcare centre just like the way she talks and sings with you at home.

Learning Story 7.6 *O le Malaga fa'alea'oa'oga a Lily Tasia in Lincoln Childcare and Preschool (part 2)*

Author: Ruta McKenzie

Conversation Stories

Learning Stories are examples of formative assessment, and in Chapter 2 we argued that they must include reference to how the learning will grow, or has grown, for example:

- a section that suggests what will improve or progress the learning (the *formative* part of the story)
- some possible next steps for progress are canvassed within the text of the story, and a further story will refer back to earlier work
- a connection is made to previous Learning Stories as a review of progress.

Portfolios of Learning Stories and examples of work are designed therefore to provide a record of a child's learning over time. However, in practice, portfolios often include a range of purposes for the documentation, not just as an assessment with respect to a wider frame. The story of a child's work or play enables conversations between children families and teachers, and sends messages about the learning that is valued here. These are interesting for families and children – especially if they include photographs or a child's art work – so they often provoke a response from the family. They keep a conversation between teachers and families going. When they include pictures, they also speak to the child; they can be the catalyst for conversations and they may become their first reader.

A magical moment

Learning Story 7.1, 'A magical moment', is an example of a *conversation story*. It is written to the father of Francesca, describing an occasion when he visited the centre. Francesca 'insisted' that her father should read the storybook planned for that time. The teacher writes with appreciation that the father included other children during his interactions, and emphasises that these important relationships between educators and families are important. It will go into Francesca's portfolio, and, in a sense, he is now 'present' at the centre, his picture and this event always available.

Super Bowl day

Learning Story 7.8, 'Super Bowl day', is about Michael and his family. Michael is in the playground and playing football – without a ball! He was pretending to hold a ball, and then to throw it to Ana, the teacher. She threw the pretend ball back, Michael jumped to get it, falling down. Another child arrived, and she became a participant in the football game. What was impressive about this story was the response from the family: an uncle, a brother, the mother, the father, and the grandfather-father. The family reflect on his football skills, and his imagination, in English and Spanish. The yard has no ball, but this does not prevent Michael from playing with an imaginary ball in a very realistic way. A student teacher responds as well. The grandfather-father tells the story of teaching Michael when he started to walk, to kick a ball, and how they watched soccer together on the television. This affirmation of his intelligence, his English language, his sporting ability and his imagination is now written down for him, and for the family, to treasure.

A magical moment

A few weeks ago, Dan, you came to pick up Francesca a bit earlier than usual. You were greeted by Francesca (of course!) but also by the other children and particularly Callum and Anya. We were about to read a book and Frankie insisted: you should be the reader! You didn't seem in a hurry so you sat down on the floor and started to read. Almost instantly, Callum and Anya came closer to you and Frankie, they were a bit unsure at first, but you gave them a beautiful smile and kept reading, interacting beautifully with them!

It seems really important to me to write this simple yet beautiful story of exchange between you, Dan and Francesca. But it is also the powerful and wonderful act of sitting down on the floor and including Frankie's friends in this very special moment that made me want to write this story for you!

As educators, we are developing strong relationships with families, but what really hit me in that moment and that we don't always realise, is that families develop relationships with other families but also with all the children in the group.

I was deeply moved by this moment and I am incredibly grateful to you Dan, to have taken the time to sit, interact and include Callum and Anya!

Thank you so much for this beautiful moment ... It might not have seemed much to you, but it meant a lot to me and to Frankie, Callum and Anya, I'm sure!

Written for Dan by a very grateful Lea!!

Learning Story 7.7   *A magical moment*

Author: Lea Gambonnet

Super Bowl Day

Michael, today when we were in the playground, I heard you calling me "Ana, Ana". You were in the sandbox. I went over there, and you stood up with your hands together, one on the top of another pretending that you were having something in them, and you said "ball". Then, you lifted one of your arms and threw me your "imaginary" ball. I caught it and I threw the ball back to you. You ran following the ball and jumped to get it, falling down on the sand. Then, you stood up and threw to me ball again. We continued the game throwing and catching the ball and after a few minutes, another child who was looking at us wanting to play and you let her take a turn with the imaginary ball. You were very patient waiting for a turn and smiling when our friend was running and falling down on the sand.

I really liked to play football with you. I could see that you love to play football, and it was a pleasure to see you smiling and laughing when you were running following the ball. But your ability to catch the ball and fall down in the sand as a professional football player was amazing!

What it means
This football play showed your imagination, gross motor skills and relationships with other children and adults. After talking with your Grandma, I see that you really enjoy going with your older brother to his football practices. You are learning a lot about this game, the way to pass the ball and to catch it and the appropriate postures. I wonder if you will be in the NFL someday. It is really special that the family spends time together, and the care Michael has for his big brother is seen within his play!

Opportunities and possibilities
Michael, to continue to support your learning, I will offer you more balls in the playground to encourage your play with other children. Maybe I can offer a real football ball, a t-shirt and arrange the yard like a football field.
Teacher Ana and in collaboration with Dr Annie White

DRDP Measures
ALT-REG 1, ALT-REG 3, SED 1, SED 3, SED 4, SED 5, LLD 1, LLD 2, LLD 3, COG 1, COG 8, COG 9, PD-HLTH 1, PD-HLTH 2, PD-HLTH 3, PD-HLTH 5

Learning Story 7.8 *Super Bowl day (part 1)*
Author: Ana Gonzalez and Annie White

Response from the family

Michael's love for football started when the family would go to his brother's high school games. Football season is very special time for our family. We go to high school games on Fridays and watch the NFL every Sundays. We are Raiders fans and their games were the first moments Michael sat still. He paid a lot of attention to the running, passing and tackling in the games. He also noticed how we would cheer during touchdowns. Soon after, he started running around with the football in hand. He asked anyone that was around to be his opponent, running until he got tackled making, all the sound effects as he fell to the ground. Every once in a while he would escape the tackle and score a touchdown. He would always celebrate by shouting "touchdown!" and throwing his hands in the air. I am amazed at how smart Michael is. He picked up every sport he has watched.
I am happy to be a part of his life and I will continue to teach him everything he wants to know.
Luis Obispo, uncle

Michael is pretty important to me ever since he arrived at the footsteps of our house. He loves football! I play for the Santa Barbara dons. He enjoyed watching the NFL programs as well. He knows that most of my family love the Oakland Raiders, he is always saying "Raiders now".
I love seeing Michael "playing football". He is always throwing himself around and throwing the ball. It is funny seeing him play because he makes a lot of sound effects as if he was a real player. I usually play with him, and when I do it he loves tackling me. But sometimes he makes me hold the ball so that he can make a "field goal".
Juan Hernandez, brother

Hello, my name is Aryzbe. I love and enjoy watching Michael play football. His favorite team is The Raiders (NFL). I love how he uses his imagination at this early age. I think it is really important.
I wonder if when he gets older, if he will continue loving football.
Thank you for the story.
Aryzbe, mother

Soy muy aficionado al football soccer y mi equipo favorito son "Las Chivas" rayadas del Guadalajara. Cuando Michael Angel llego a nosotros y yo lo cuidaba, siempre estaba sentado en el sillon frente al televisor, quiza pore so Angel le gusta. Cuando empezo a caminar, empece a ensenarle como patear el balon y aprendio muy rapido, entonces empezamos a ensenarle otros deportes y en poco tiempo aprendio como jugarlos. El es muy inteligente y en su forma de hablar nos da a entender que es lo que quiere ya sea comer, jugar o las cosas que desea. Estoy muy contento con Angel que se ha ganado mi carino y corazon.
Tomas Obispo, grandfather-father

English interpretation
I am a soccer fan and my favorite team is "Las Chivas" Rayadas from Guadalajara, Mexico. When Michael Angel came to us, I used to take care of him. I was constantly sitting on the sofa in front of the television set. Perhaps that is why Angel likes soccer. When he started to walk, I began to teach him how to kick the soccer ball. He quickly learned how to do it. We then started to teach him about other sports, and he learned to play them in a very short time. He is very intelligent and by the way he talks, he lets us know what he needs; whether it is eating, playing or any other desire. I am very happy that Angel has gained my love and my heart.
Tomas Obispo, Grandfather-father

Response from California State University, Channel Islands Student Teacher:
Michael, when I witnessed this within the yard and heard your teacher describe how significant this event was it was truly heart-warming! I could see how wonderful this play was for you and how excited you were to throw the ball with Ana! You really knew all of the moves! Thank you for this wonderful experience of watching you grow and learn. I hope you continue to play many games throughout your life! With your enthusiasm and love for sports, I wonder if you will grow up and play on a sports team!
Toni

This Learning Story includes mandated developmental assessment required by the funding agency for this Head Start program

Learning Story 7.8 *Super Bowl day (part 2)*

Authors: Luis Obispo, Juan Hernandez, Maria Obispo, Aryzbe, Thomas Obispo and Toni

Learner identities cross boundaries

Chapter 3 in this book described the inclusion of being *willing* (as well as being ready and being able) in the definition of a learning disposition. We noted that learning dispositions are sensitive to place and surrounding opportunity, so they will be more likely to flourish in one place than in another. This is because enabling or disabling opportunities are context dependent. This provides an opportunity for counter-perspectives and a plurality of identities – a fertile ground for creative thinking as learners contemplate the differences. But it is also, maybe, a fertile ground for confusion if discussions about difference are avoided. Etienne Wenger, in his book on *Communities of Practice* (1998: 160–161), adds a comment that is relevant to this discussion:

> I am suggesting that the maintenance of an identity across boundaries requires work ... This work is not simply an additional concern for an independently defined identity viewed as a unitary object; rather, it is at the core of what it means to be a person.

In a book from a research project entitled *Crossing the Border: A Community Negotiates the Transition from Early Childhood to Primary School* (Hartley et al., 2012), the researchers report on what happened when children took their early childhood portfolios with them to school. One child, Gaurav, was very reluctant to communicate with the other children or the teacher, and the teacher suggested to his family that he bring his early childhood portfolio to the school classroom. Suddenly, Gaurav had a boundary object that became a resource for communication and belonging on his own terms. The teacher commented:

> I would turn around at all times of the day and hear little murmurings and laughing and there would be pockets of children sitting around this little boy with his kindergarten book. (Hartley et al., 2012: 25; see also Peters et al., 2009)

Exploring at a snail's pace

What makes Learning Story 7.9, 'Exploring at a snail's pace', a Learning Story, designed to enable learning that connects with home, is the key question: 'Does Lee show an interest in insects at home?' In Chapter 2 we wrote of the ABCDE of progress, as five ways in which the learning is strengthened and will move forward. The teacher recognises that an interest is strengthened if 'Breadth' is encouraged, if stronger and more diverse connections are made with family and community funds of knowledge (and disposition). If an interest, in this case snails, is in more than one place, it might be said that the interest disconnects from being an interest in the snail as it leaves a trail on the wooden plank *on one occasion* and *in one place*, to becoming an interest in snails and their trails – at home, elsewhere, in books or on the footpath. When we talk about a 'learner identity', these are the contexts which enable learning dispositions to grow.

Exploring at a snail's pace

Documented by Jessica Coombe

This week, the tamariki have shown a real interest in snails. Today, during a cloudy spring morning, a group of tamariki noticed three snails slowly crawling up a wooden plank. We watched the snails slowly but steadily move in different directions leaving a trail behind them. They moved left, right, backwards, forwards and round and round.

Lee initially watched from afar but came in for a closer look once the other tamariki had moved on. Trish and I talked to Lee about the snail's textures, movements and trails. Lee was so fascinated that she went in for a closer look.

What learning did I observe?

Trish and I stepped back and marvelled in Lee's pleasure of discovery. She sustained an interest for a long period of time. She was respectful and showed such hāmārika (gentleness) for these living creature as she gave them space to move.

Whether it hops, crawls, runs, wriggles, slithers, swims, flies, buzzes or chirrups look after it. Human beings needs nature!

Does Lee show an interest in insects at home?

How might we stretch Lee's learning?

From here, I will continue to introduce Lee to the small creatures in the playground. I will model hāmārika (gentleness) and whakaute (respect) and use these opportunities to enhance Lee's repertoire of descriptive words.

Learning Story 7.9 *Exploring at a snail's pace*

Author: Jessica Coombe

As we have shown in previous chapters, families have occasionally contributed stories from home to their child's portfolio, and these promote connections with the centre. Sometimes families are shy or feel inadequate to do this. In a project on family engagement in a kindergarten (Clarkin-Phillips and Carr, 2014) the teachers constructed 'kindy book bags' for the portfolio, a parallel to the local school's 'reading book bags' that regularly went home from the new entrant classroom with a reading book. These were familiar to the families with older children at school, and the similar 'packing' encouraged them to take it home and for someone at home – often a grandparent – to revisit, talk about and contribute a story, often hand-written, from home. Photographs of family and of pets in the assessment portfolio provide a vehicle for a sense of belonging in this place, and it is not unusual for centres to arrange for a family to borrow a camera to do this.

Keeping learning in the foreground: the use of both paper-based and e-portfolios

Opportunities to write stories and insert photographs digitally have revolutionised the making of Learning Stories. They have extended the range of feedback about learning to reify (make visible and 'concrete') a learner as a learner-plus for a wide community of interest. Learning Stories become available to the teachers in cooperative early childhood education contexts, as well as to parents and grandparents.

Both of the authors of this book remember when Learning Stories were written by hand, or typed up and photographs glued on. The roll of photographic negatives of photographs was sent to the local chemist for printing, which usually took a week or ten days. Then, how excited the teachers were when polaroid cameras were invented! 'It's so instant!', commented a teacher. But the polaroid photographs still had to be physically attached to the story, and they slowly discoloured over time. Now, however, the digital camera or phone is linked to the computer or printer, allowing direct and regular communications across media and communities.

A research project, researching the integration of ICT into everyday learning and teaching in the kindergarten in a multicultural and multilingual community,[1] introduced 'Welcome Stories' and enabled children to take their own photographs. The project introduced 'Welcome Stories' to families on day one of a child's attendance (Ramsey et al., 2006: 19). Here is one example:

> *Che starts kindergarten*. After he had been introduced to his file [portfolio] and the first-day (Welcome) story in it, on the second day he asked to borrow a camera; a teacher taught him how to use it, and he photographed his file [portfolio] on the shelf, the first page of the file, and his Welcome Story. A second Story was written, with his photos included, as well as photographs of Che taking photographs and sharing them with another child.

Today, some centres provide Learning Stories online, and families access them by mobile phone or computer and are able to send them on to families who live at a distance. ICT is now a valued integral part of the communication with families in the ECE sector.

Paper-based and e-portfolios

E-portfolios – Learning Stories regularly sent to families via the internet – are increasingly common. We are advocates for both paper-based and e-portfolios: both are essential but for different reasons. We suggest that there are eight considerations.

Reflections on the audience and the authority. Paper-based portfolios are critical for young children whereas e-portfolios are designed primarily for adults (i.e. parents and family). The idea of only having an e-portfolio for young children in early childhood settings undermines one of the purposes and principles of formative assessment: that children will become accustomed to engage in self-assessment. It ignores the fact that when paper-based portfolios are readily available in the centre or classroom, the portfolio has the power to support, construct and reify the learner identity for the owner. Research by Tracey Hooker (2015: 21) in one centre recorded the ways in which one teacher was including the child's voice in their e-portfolio:

> When I am working with children, I use the tablet and e-portfolio to document the childrens voice as they share their ideas with me. For example, I have documented a child's voice towards four paintings they had done. It highlights the story behind their work. ….. Recently a family put holiday photos on their child's e-portfolio. I took an opportunity to revisit these photos with the child and then I recorded his voice and gave him time to share these photos with me. (Leslie, teacher, midway survey, March 2014)

Conversations and understandings. Paper-based Learning Stories are readily available for revisiting and sharing at any time. They enable children and adults to discuss the learning using the paper-based portfolio as a prompt and this enables a collaborative conversation about progress and what might come next. The paper-based portfolio is accessible at all times (see Learning Story 1.1, where two children are reading the photographs to revisit the events in their portfolios). The learning journey can be readily traced through the photographs and the re-reading and re-visiting.

Learning Stories as literacy and language artefacts. Even very young children can 'read' the photographs of their learning experiences, and many children learn part of the script by heart. They may have dictated some of the text. Research indicates that children are more involved in contributing to their paper-based portfolio when the portfolios are accessible and participation is encouraged (Goodman and Cherrington, 2015). There is developing evidence too of the value for the development of early oral language skill of shared paper-based portfolio revisiting by children and teachers, particularly when the interaction takes a 'reminiscing' approach (i.e. the portfolio is used as a prompt for children's personal narratives) (Reese et al. 2019).

Combining language and text. Learning Stories are engaging documents that invite children in. They are vital literacy artefacts for the young child. We are not talking about 'decorating the Learning Story', but about the way in which images and text can combine in the Learning Story to engage and invite the child in. Just as picture books are inviting and engaging, so too do we want the portfolio – paper-based or e-portfolio – to be both inviting and engaging. Paper-based portfolios are books that are often valued in the family for many years; they retain their capacity to encourage excitement, enthusiasm and enjoyment in their descriptions of a competent and confident learner (see Carr & Lee, 2012).

In digital format, Learning Stories can travel to family members outside the home. The stories about learning reach out to and connect families, often grandparents, in many countries. E-portfolios have a distinct place in providing families with immediate access to the child's learning and activities, enabling learning interests and activities to be connected across the 'borders' between home and school.

Speed and ease of communication. E-portfolios are valued for the speed and ease of communicating children's learning to the parents and family. The immediate access into the parents' mobile phone, for example, 'means sharing and communicating between parents and family members can be more frequent and meaningful, and this communication has resulted in improved learning outcomes for children' (Goodman and Cherrington, 2015: 12). There is no doubt that parents value the immediacy of the digital platform and the ability to connect both locally and globally with wider family members.

When the format for analysing the learning in an e-portfolio is fixed and narrowly prescribed, the teacher voice is denied. Recent developments towards proforma e-portfolio formats encourage teachers to tick learning tags as the analysis of the learning episode or activity. These diminish the professional role of the teacher as a thoughtful and knowledgeable analyst of the learning. They can deny the vital opportunity for the teacher to tentatively and collaboratively enable the learner to recognise some possible next steps and how to take them.

Opportunities of ready-to-hand software platforms benefit both paper-based and e-portfolios. The use of software such as Pages on a Mac or Comic Life on both a Mac and PC allows the process of developing a Learning Story quickly, but maintains the attraction of the child and family to the story and its meaning. This is one of the important strengths of technology.

As Lorraine Sands, a professional learning facilitator with the Educational Leadership Project, comments: 'Proformas are flat, lifeless versions of Learning Stories. Learning is made visible when Learning Stories are wrapped around each child's learning context. This requires emotional connection through photos and contextual writing that show learning continuity and "speak to children and families" of the child they know and love' (personal communication).

It is not a question of either e-portfolios or a paper-based portfolio. Both are useful. Case studies in two ECE settings by the New Zealand Ministry of Education in 2014 indicated that e-portfolios were valuable 'as a complement to not a replacement for, the usual paper-based portfolios' (Hooker, 2015: 19). It is not enough to photograph an event and then describe it. If we are to have an impact on engaging families' and parents' aspirations for their children, we need to thoughtfully connect the learning episode to the individual child, to his or her learning progress and to powerful frameworks.

In summary, paper-based portfolios are the foundation of effective assessment for young children in early childhood settings and e-portfolios have greatly enhanced family engagement in their children's learning. Both are useful, even necessary, but their use needs to be carefully constructed to keep the child's learning in the foreground. 'What is becoming increasingly clear is that kids today don't need better gadgets to get ahead in our uber-competitive high-tech world – they need sharper minds' (Kardaras, 2016: 33). If children have opportunities to develop sharper minds and to voice their opinions in their early years they will be well prepared to face the technological challenges of the twenty-first century. A connected and thoughtful portfolio of Learning Stories, in either a paper-based format or in both formats, will be a very important part of this journey.

Recognise family aspirations

In the 2012 book on Learning Stories, we cited John Hattie's research on family aspirations. His 2009 survey (Hattie, 2009: 70) of research in education concluded that 'Across all home variables, parental aspirations and expectations for children's educational achievement has the strongest relationship with achievement'. On the same page, John Hattie warned:

> Parents have major effects in terms of the encouragement and expectations that they transmit to their children. Many parents, however, struggle to comprehend the language of learning and thus are disadvantaged in the methods that they use to encourage their children to attain their expectations.

Learning Stories and portfolios can contribute to families acquiring some of these languages of learning, expectations and methods to encourage children through the ways that they (i) write Learning Stories and develop portfolios, and (ii) highlight the learning dispositions that are valuable for later education and life. Portfolios also invite examples or comments from home, and families occasionally support growing learning dispositions (including the skills and knowledge) that have been identified in a portfolio – especially if they are referenced as valuable for learning now and in the future (at school, for instance).

A publication in te reo Māori (translated into English), *Te Whatu Pōkeka*, includes Kaupapa Māori Learning and Assessment Exemplars from five of the many early childhood centres in New Zealand where the Māori language only is spoken (New Zealand MoE, 2009). These examples are analysed in terms of Māori kaupapa or philosophy as *Nga hononga ki te tauparapara*: Ways of knowing; *Ngāāhuatanga o te tamaiti*: Ways of being; and *Tikanga whakaako*: Ways of doing. This publication is referenced in Learning Story 7.10.

Your special taonga

Learning Story 7.10, 'Your special taonga', is a story about Tyson and an artefact; it is also about kaupapa Māori (Māori philosophy) and a whānau (family in the widest sense) story. It was initiated four weeks earlier by Tyson, when he shared his pounamu stone that his grandparents gave to him with the teacher, and she shared her own. The teacher and Tyson searched online for images of greenstone carvings, and Tyson paints a koru (spiral pattern), adding a line that turns it into what he names as a 'koru lollipop'. He shares his painting with his grandparents when they visit; they write a whānau voice/comment about how they recognised that the pounamu 'had finally found its way home'. They add:

> Look into the taonga and you will see Tyson there. The shape signifies Tyson's creativity, passion and energy. The marble colouring holds proud his blended Māori, European and Niuean heritage. His strength and courage, his compassion and empathy are the rigidity and texture of the pounamu. The taonga is special because our moko makes it so.[2]

Flying in an airplane

The *observation* in Learning Story 7.11, 'Flying in an airplane', is a vivid example of a person-plus. Demetrius is the person; his pillows are the constant plus. The teacher writes a comment in her analysis ('What it means') that makes it clear to the family that she is happy with this arrangement and she will always make sure that the pillows are available for Demetrius. In this particular story, the wooden airplane is also a plus to which he returns in between group activities. It enables him to be the key player in a storyline of 'Flying in an airplane'. *Opportunities and possibilities* are included: the teacher's observations over time have indicated to her that Demetrius loves to sing and dance, so she will provide plenty more opportunities for this. In a way, this is a story about belonging, and the person-plus definition of a learner is central to belonging as a construct. The *parent response* is written to Demetrius, indicating in print that his mother knows how he feels, and predicting that school will get more comfortable for him.

Your special taonga

Tyson, a few weeks ago I clearly remember you vibrantly sharing with me your really special taonga - your greenstone necklace. Over the last four weeks, I have had a student called Tukimihia here with us learning to be a teacher and when she left she gave me a really special taonga, just like yours. Today (9.6.14) I brought my pounamu in to show you, so we could share in meaningful discussions about our gifts.

You carefully open the box to my necklace and said "can I put it on?" "yes, you can" I replied. "Your one is not the same as my one, my one is this shape and your one is this shape but it matches mine." You then continued to say "my one came from Nanny and Pop, found it from the greenstone and they picked it up and they gave it to me, and they put lots of lollies in it and I eat them in my tummy." [Nanny and Pop, I would love to hear more about this story of how you "found "or picked Tyson's pounamu]
As we sat together, you were analysing each of the pounamu and I asked you "what does your greenstone mean I wonder Tyson?" You replied, "it means that it is special and that I am special."

Together, we then delved into meaningful research as we searched online for images of greenstone carvings and you said "I can paint that." You sat patiently at the art easel, moving the brush to the rhythm of your ideas. You began with the circle shapes - "this is a koru" you tell me. Then comes the orange line, "the stick, this is a koru lollipop". You then painted the blue lines, "this is a koru lollipop, with the amazing sun".

What really makes this story special to me too Tyson, was in the afternoon your Nanny and Pop arrived with your Mum to collect you. You were so excited to see them and you took Pop to show him your picture, which was on the wall.

Ehara taku toa I te toa takitahi engari he toa takitini
I come not with my own strengths but bring with me
gifts, talents and strengths of my family, tribe and
ancestors

Learning Story 7.10 *Your special taonga (part 1)*
Author: Karen Goldsworthy

Tyson, over the last week I have attended professional development teaching me about the principles of Te Whatu Pōkeka and what it means to be Māori learner. I have been reflective upon what I have learnt Tyson, thinking about how I can apply it to this story...

Ngā hononga ki te tauparapara: Ways of knowing
Mōhiotanga

Tyson, you have a strong understanding of the importance and value your necklace holds as you proudly wear it everyday. You told me your grandparents gave it to you because 'it is special and I am special'. You are Tyson – you are a unique person with your own mana, mauri and wairua inherited through your ancestors, therefore your very being is treasured (Te Whatu Pōkeka).

Ngā āhuatanga o te tamaiti: Ways of being
He mauri tangata

"Mauri is the observable. It is the life force and energy of the child, which enables energy to be expended· the mind to think and have some control over how the body behaves. It enables the child to be vibrant, expressive and impressive." (He Pou Tātāki).
When I reflect upon this saying Tyson, I am taken back to your moment of painting and I know your Mauri or life force is healthy - you painted such a thoughtful painting, expressive of our conversation and vibrant in detail. You confidently articulated what this painting represented and you actively participated in your own learning and understanding.

Tikanga whakaaro: Ways of doing

"Learning and teaching within the Māori context is based on whanaungatanga and tikanga Māori, the Māori word 'ako' means both learning and teaching" (Te Whatu Pōkeka).
Tyson, over time and through meaningful interactions and play we have come to build a reciprocal trusting relationship. As a teacher I am not the expert, rather we are learning beside each other as we share ideas, construct knowledge and explore our understandings of the world around us in meaningful ways. Sharing our taonga was special to me Tyson and I thank you for giving me the opportunity to further strengthen our connection.

Whānau Voice / Comments
19/06/2014 – Dean Te Tai (SNR)
What a thoughtful account Karen thanks for sharing it with us. The easiest way to explain how Tyson's pounamu came to be is to simply say... it chose him. We searched far and wide and examined dozens possibly hundreds of stones, looking for that "special something" initially without much success. We finally stopped in a little place in Kawakawa and as we looked through their selection of stones nanny said "here he is" and held up the taonga. There was no need for examination or consultation as we knew it had finally found its way home. Look into the taonga and you will see Tyson there. The shape signifies Tyson's creativity passion and energy The marble colouring holds proud his blended Maori, European and Niuen heritage. His strength and courage, his compassion and empathy are the rigidity and texture of the pounamu. The taonga is special because our moko makes it so.

20/06/2014 – Freda Te Tai
I think Tyson has pretty much summed it up, a special gift for a very special boy, I think it's more about Tyson and not so much the pounamu. I really had no idea it would, and does mean so much to him. He wears it with such pride and I am so proud of him.

Learning Story 7.10 *Your special taonga (part 2)*
Author: Karen Goldsworthy

Flying in an Airplane

Observation

It was in the morning during free play, when I looked over and saw you carrying two pillows. I asked you if you were going on a trip and you smiled at me. I said, "Okay, Demetrius, you are all packed and ready to go and now all you have to do is board the plane!" You and I both giggled and I pointed to our wooden airplane made out of big carpeted blocks. You walked over to the plane and carefully got into the pilot's seat. You put one pillow on the side of the plane and kept the other one with you for comfort. You jumped a couple times and we sang the Jumping song, "Jump, Jump little Demetrius, Jump, Jump, little Demetrius, Jump, Jump little Demetrius, while we sing this song" ☺ which made you smile! After the Jumping song, you sat down in the airplane and put your hands on the wheel. I said, "Bye Demetrius, fly safe!" You then started turning the wheel while sitting on your pillow. You were smiling and stayed in the little plane until it was time to start another activity.

What it means

Demetrius, it is so nice to see that you have found a way to comfort yourself when you are feeling a little sensitive at school. You always find your pillows here at school and carry them around, soothing yourself. It was so nice to see you enjoying yourself in the airplane! You were smiling at me and engaging me in your play, you have a great smile! Your social skills are improving day by day!

Opportunities and possibilities

Since you love to sing and dance, I will make sure you have plenty of opportunities to do just that! We have a dance party every morning after we sing at circle time and I will keep encouraging you to dance and sing with your classmates! Now that I know you are soothed by holding pillows, I will make sure that they are always available to you, so you are comfortable! I will also continue to make sure that you have plenty of small group activities, so you can continue to be comfortable and make new friends here at school!

Parent response

Dear Demetrius,

Mommy loves your airplane. I wish I was there to have gone on the trip with you. I had school, but I hope we can do this on the weekend when it's our days together. I also love to see that you are enjoying school just like Mommy. School has its scary moments, but I promise you that it will get more comfortable for you. You will make friends with classmates as well as your teachers. I love that you are using your pillows to feel safe while Mommy is making a better life for the both of us. I love you baby boy!! Keep up the good work!! Mommy is proud!

Love,

Mommy

Learning Story 7.11 *Flying in an airplane*

Author: Noeline Robinson and Marquita S. Covington (Mom)

Further thinking

1. Reflect on John Hattie's comment about the importance of family expectations. What are some key elements of Learning Stories that might strengthen this recognition of learning?
2. Develop an argument about the difference between e-portfolios and paper-based versions. Consider this in the educational context that you know best.

Further reading

Carr, Margaret and Lee, Wendy (2012) *Learning Stories: Constructing Learner Identities in Early Education*. London: SAGE. Chapter 4: Making connections across boundaries between places.

Hartley, Carol; Rogers, Pat; Smith, Jemma; Peters, Sally and Carr, Margaret (2012) *Crossing the Border: A Community Negotiates the Transition from Early Childhood to Primary School*. Wellington New Zealand: NZCER Press

New Zealand Ministry of Education (2004) *Kei tua o te Pae* Book 5 – *Community*. Downloadable at: www.education.govt.nz/assets/Documents/Early-Childhood/Kei-Tua-o-te-Pae/ECEBooklet5Full.pdf (3 December 2018).

Note

1. This was a Centre of Innovation project, funded by the Ministry of Education; these projects were initiated by the teachers in an early childhood centre, who then invited a researcher or researchers to assist them to tackle their chosen research questions. Examples from a number of these projects are in *Constructing Learner Identities in Early Education* (Carr and Lee, 2012).

taonga = Treasure

tangata = person, man, human being, individual

whakaaro = to think, plan, consider, decide

Kaupapa Māori = A Māori approach that assumes the normalcy of being Māori – language, customs, knowledge, principles, ideology, agenda

whanaungatanga = Kinship, sense of whānau connection – a relationship through shared experiences and working together that provides people with a sense of belonging

moko = mokopuna, grandchild

8

Constructing Progress

In Reggio they have questioned and rethought. In one of his speeches, Loris Malaguzzi talked about their idea of knowledge as a 'tangle of spaghetti'. Carlina [Rinaldi] takes a similar view when she says that 'learning does not proceed in a linear way, determined and deterministic, by progressive and predictable stages, but rather is constructed through contemporaneous advances, standstills, and "retreats" that take many directions'. (Carlina Rinaldi, 2006: 131–132)

> # Key messages
>
> - Measuring learning over time
> - Developing communicative expertise: becoming literate and numerate
> - Learning Stories connect a journey

Measuring learning over time

Measuring

We see from the quote at the beginning of this chapter that, on one occasion, the first pedagogical director of the Reggio Emilia municipal schools, Loris Malaguzzi, described knowledge as a 'tangle of spaghetti'. In Chapter 5 we argued that one of the assessment tasks for teachers is to manage ambiguity and uncertainty, and the metaphor of learning in the early years as a 'tangle' invites us now to try to make the topic of *progress* less uncertain. We agree with Carlina Rinaldi that there are advances, standstills, and 'retreats' that take many directions. However, since our 2012 book, *Constructing Learner Identities in Early Education*, the cry for accountability has included, in many countries, an insistence on robust descriptions of learning improvement. Governments are keen on measures and, in our view, we have to see this as an interesting challenge to have a conversation about. Measuring, in our case of storying, does not mean numbers or levels. Our *Collins English Dictionary* (1992: 969) defines 'to measure' as 'to assess the nature, character, quality, etc. of someone or something'. As a noun, 'a measure' is described as a *system* of measurement. With this in mind, Learning Stories are measures. The 'nature, character or quality' of a learning episode is in the analysis of the learning in the Learning Story. The analysis and the 'What next?' or 'How can we grow this learning?', etc. sections are integral to the Learning Story system.

The growth of a learner-self: chains of 'flow' episodes and learning dispositions

The portfolios in which Learning Stories are housed provide a measure of the growing of learning dispositions, skills and knowledge: a learner-self. In the final chapter of the 2012 Learning Story book we wrote about Mihaly Csikszentmihalyi's notion of the 'flow experience' and his version of creativity and continuity as chains of 'flow' episodes. In his book, *Finding Flow*, Csikszentmihalyi (1997: 30) has written about the affective nature of the experience of 'flow': when someone, or a group of people, is 'fully involved in overcoming a challenge that is just about manageable'. This involvement in overcoming a challenge is one of key learning dispositions. Another is the disposition to make a contribution: in Chapter 3 we described the hopes and dreams of new parents for the future of their soon-to-be-born child; a key feature was that children would contribute to their local community, and that the community would enable this. An early childhood centre and a classroom provide spaces in which this learning disposition can be nurtured and grow. It includes agency, kindness, friendship, 'reading' an environment in order to make a contribution. Teachers will have their own list of dispositions; often set out in a curriculum. In his 1993 book, *The Evolving Self*, Csikszentmihalyi cites one of the learning dispositions that is strengthened when learning is 'in flow': recognising a way to assess how well one is doing.

> And every flow experience contributes to the growth of the self. To be in flow, one has to formulate intentions, and have a way to assess how well one is doing. The self is made up mainly of information about goals and feedback. Therefore after every episode involving flow, we are a little different from what we were before. (Csikszentmihalyi, 1993: 237)

Developing communicative expertise: becoming literate and numerate

Reframing literacy and numeracy as part of a wider tangle of communicative and dispositional expertise

In the first years of school, literacy and numeracy loom large, often set out in a linear way and divided into increasingly complex skills and understandings, which can be readily observed and assessed early in the school year, and sometimes during the preschool years. They are often described as early decoding of letters and words, counting and calculating. We suggest that numeracy and literacy are just two of a cluster of 'languages' or modes of communication where the purpose and the disposition is to communicate and to make sense of the world in a range of ways. This cluster is growing in the early years as well as across the lifespan because it is immediately and immensely purposeful and powerful. The general term for the cluster that we highlight here is *semiotics*: communicating and making meaning using various modes. We have listed some of them, as a semiotic array:

i   Using and hearing spoken language for a purpose
ii Reading signs and recognising their meaning
iii Recognising and using numbers and shapes as patterns and quantities, useful for problem-setting and solving; understanding how 'bits' work together to make a whole
iv Recognising artefacts and art that can communicate ideas for which spoken language is not required or adequate
v   Constructing with building materials for spatial design and opportunities for collaboration

vi   Recognising rhythm and rhyme in music, and written words in poetry and
     stories for joy and pleasure
vii Recognising gestures (including photographing) as unspoken communication.

We suggest that being ready, willing and able to recognise and communicate with
these modes, and the resources that facilitate them, is also a key task of early
childhood and school and that it enables an expansion of ways of thinking and
creative engagement with the world. This connects to the argument for possible
and creative thinking that was introduced in Chapter 5.

Portfolios of Learning Stories are able to document and comment on the development of these semiotic dispositions, including the skills and intentions that are
attached to them. Their growth cannot be assessed by 'measuring' in just the narrow numerical sense. Here we look back on the Learning Stories in Chapters 2 to
7 in this book, and we invite the reader to return to look at them in this light: as
a semiotic array of communicative thinking. They are listed here without the
accompanying portfolios that would include follow-on and prior comments and
stories. The Learning Stories documented the children becoming more capable
and expert at:

i.   Using and hearing spoken language for a purpose:
      2.7   Butterfly getting eaten!
      4.3   He Kaikōrero Māori/A Māori language speaker
      6.4   Hold my hand
      6.5   The group leader

ii.   Reading signs and recognising their meaning:
      2.3   Nature girl
      3.1   Literacy in the bush
      3.8   Akari's challenge
      6.7   Developing a love of literacy
      7.7   A magical moment

iii. Recognising and using numbers and shapes as patterns and quantities, useful
      for problem-setting and solving; understanding how 'bits' work together to
      make a whole:
      2.1   Handyman to the rescue
      2.9   Huddy hammering
      3.4   It's tricky!
      5.1   A tree, some apples and a dog
      5.10 Logical and creative thinking!
      6.1   Grayson adds, divides and compares

iv   Recognising artefacts and art that can communicate ideas for which spoken
      language is not required or adequate:
      5.2   Poet loves paint
      6.3   Layers of black: the varied canvas of a busy painter

6.6 Drawing hands

6.8 Finding wonderment in the rainbow fish!

7.10 Your special taonga

v Constructing with building materials for spatial design and opportunities for collaboration:

5.4 The builders

5.6 No more room

5.7 Being proud of one's work

vi Recognising rhythm and rhyme in music, and written words in poetry and stories for joy and pleasure:

3.2 Puff the Magic Dragon

3.6 Elsie is a pattern maker!

4.1 A story reading performer

6.9 Purerehua butterfly

vii Recognising gestures (including photographing) as unspoken communication:

4.2 Courage

4.4 My learner identity

5.9 Shared interests across different languages

7.8 Super Bowl day

viii Learning continues at home

5.8 Real and pretend maps

8.3 Embracing a challenge

8.4 A story from home

ix Illustrating progress in activities (within stories and in stories over time)

4.5 Dad, me and spider

7.1 Weaving and more

7.2 French knitting

7.3 Making connections

These nine semiotic modes are about children *being able* to recognise, read and use signs and symbols, both spoken and written. We emphasise that, in practice, they are accompanied by, *tangled with*, being *ready* and *willing* to communicate in these ways. The Learning Stories do this. This is one way of interpreting Malaguzzi's 'tangle of spaghetti' metaphor in the quote that opened this chapter.

Learning Stories connect a journey: a case study

A 'progressive filter' of the Learning Story assessment process, pictured below, was introduced in Chapter 1. It describes progression too. Teachers are noticing, recognising and responding to the children's learning many, many times during any one day at the early childhood, or early years, centre. Some of those occasions will be written down, recorded, as Learning Stories for portfolios. And many Learning Stories will be revisited by teachers during team discussions, by teachers with the children, by children on their own and with each other, and by families. Revisiting and reviewing will seldom be recorded, but written comments and connected examples from families will be stored in the portfolios.

Below we include a selection of Learning Stories from a portfolio that includes all six of these progressive (noticing through to reviewing) processes. This is a small selection of the Learning Stories for Gideon, who arrived at a kindergarten at age three-and-a-half, and went to school at age five.

Example one: social interactions
A working relationship

Learning Story 8.1, 'A working relationship', is an early Learning Story for Gideon, an example of two children 'constructing with building materials for spatial design and opportunities for collaboration' (see (v), above). There was no verbal language and the teacher writes that 'you were able to convey your ideas together through non-verbal gestures'. They are recognising that buckets and sand can communicate ideas for which spoken language is not required or adequate (see (iv), above). Of course there is more than dimensions of semiotics here: this is a comfortable place for Gideon. He is willing to be there because it is not crowded and he loves working with sand. The commentary from the teacher unpacks the collaboration: to listen to another's idea, take turns and share ideas.

A Working Relationship

Kim

This morning I was in the sandpit with Aaira, helping her to make some sandcastles. Gideon, you noticed that the first sandcastle we had made was broken on one side and this was to be the beginning of a great working relationship as you gathered another bucket and began to fill it with sand.

Aaira helped to add some sand too and after you had patted the sand down, you then tipped your bucket over. Gideon, previously you had helped Aaira to stomp on the sandcastle, and this is what the two of you did together with the latest sandcastle you had built. 'Stomp, stomp, stomp', I said as the two of you squashed the sandcastle.

This had you smiling and you and Aaira were soon busy filling another bucket. When the sand was close to the top of the bucket, you would pat it down and then Aaira would add some more sand. Although there was no verbal language spoken, you were able to convey your ideas together through non-verbal gestures. This was great team work!

Gideon, with the bucket full of sand, you decided it was time to tip it over. Patting the base of the bucket, you then carefully lifted the bucket up to reveal another sandcastle.

Once again you and Aaira stomped and stomped to squash the sandcastle, and then you were back working together to fill the bucket and create another sandcastle.

Gideon, you and Aaira continued to play together for quite some time, what a fun way to spend a morning at kindergarten.

What learning do I see happening for Gideon

It was great to see Gideon initiating and maintaining a working relationship with Aaira this morning. Aaira is new to kindergarten and Gideon was a kind friend this morning as he worked with Aaira. Gideon was the leader as he directed Aaira through non-verbal communication and they worked together on a common interest of creating sandcastles. There was a fun aspect to this relationship as the ultimate experience was to be able to stomp the sandcastles, creating smiles and a sense of camaraderie as Gideon and Aaira worked collaboratively. It is important to be able to listen to another's idea, to take turns, and to share ideas; this is developing social competency, and is important for developing friendships. Through this interaction Gideon was sharing his expertise as he took on the role of the expert, very capably building the sandcastles, and Aaira was the learner as she worked with Gideon to fill the buckets.

Gideon, it was exciting to see you initiating contact and working collaboratively with Aaira. You sustained your interest in creating sandcastles and you were a learning companion as you worked with Aaira and helped her to be successful. This is being a kind friend Gideon, and at Roskill South we believe this is certainly an important disposition to foster. We will continue to encourage you to be involved and to grow responsive and reciprocal relationships by supporting your interactions with the other children.

Learning Story 8.1 *A working relationship*

Author: Kim Parkinson

Collaboration

Learning Story 8.2, 'Collaboration', is another collaborative sand play episode some months later. In this case, the sand play is much more complex. A cooperative project is being constructed, and the teacher-writer emphasises the curriculum strand 'Exploration', which takes the analysis beyond the social. Here, the children are planning and decision-making verbally, each of them contributing to a joint enterprise, and adding an imaginative storyline.

Example two: tackling a challenge

Embracing a challenge

Learning Story 8.3, 'Embracing a challenge', is an important story about progression. The monkey bars are often a feature of early childhood playgrounds. They establish a challenge as a person-plus: the learner and the resource (in this case, a piece of equipment) become the unit of analysis. Resources in early childhood are often designed to present a challenge – sometimes the challenge has a right answer (like a jigsaw). In this case the success can be measured by the player: *how far* equals *how many rungs* can the learner master before she or he falls off. In this case, Gideon had been working away for several days. His progress is recorded in the story, also his technique. This story includes progression inside the Learning Story: it includes Gideon working away on this challenge. A week later he changes the play equipment to see if this makes a difference. The teacher comments on his enthusiasm and his 'can do' attitude.

A story from home

Learning Story 8.4, 'A story from home', is a story from home about Gideon tackling a Flying Fox at a park. He was thrown off it, and said he would never want to get onto any Flying Fox. Then, his mother reports, 'His monkey bar challenge Learning Story came to my mind'. She reminded him of his gradual success, his perseverance ('How many times did you fall to the ground … ?'). Two days later, Gideon went back to the same Flying Fox.

Example three: patterning
A caterpillar design

Gideon has become very interested in making mosaic tiles. Learning Story 8.5, 'A caterpillar design', reminds him of a previous occasion when he completed an abstract design; the teacher then suggests that he increase the difficulty by trying a picture design.

COLLABORATION

Kim

Gideon, this morning you had noticed Fraser working in the sandpit digging a channel for the water to flow through, and you offered to lend a hand. You watched as Fraser collected some of the wooden logs from behind the shed door to create a bridge and as you continued to dig the channel Paora and Fraser lay the logs across the river.

Work continued, and Gideon you then helped Fraser gather the logs, placing them side by side as the three of you worked together just like a construction crew! Fraser took on the role of the planner, directing and advising you and Paora of where the logs should be placed, making sure the logs were placed side by side, and overseeing the digging to ensure the water would run smoothly down the river.

Time to stand back and critique the placement of the logs, with Fraser declaring that you had now created no ordinary bridge, in fact it was a train track bridge! "There's a crocodile in the water", he shouted as he tipped a bucket of water into the river.

This had you all scrambling to dig a bigger hole and while Paora, took on the role of the crocodile watcher, you ensured the river was deep enough as you helped Fraser to dig deeper. There was a lovely sense of camaraderie as you and your friends worked together, sharing ideas and changing roles as the need arose.

WHAT LEARNING DO I SEE HAPPENING FOR GIDEON

Gideon, you were keen to join in and help Fraser with his plan confidently offering your help, and keen to be part of the 'construction crew'. Laying the logs across the river required some thoughtful direction and management, and Gideon you worked collaboratively with Fraser and Paora, knowing that your involvement was an important role to achieving the goal of creating a flowing river and bridge. Through your exploration, Gideon, and your passion to be involved you were contributing to the needs and wellbeing of your friends, accepting their ideas and enjoying the relationships you were forming with Fraser and Paora. Gideon, this whakatāukī came to mind as I watched you working with your friends, and I could see that your contribution was valued by Fraser and Paora too.

Ehara taku toa i te toa takitahi, engari he toa takitini ke.
Cooperation of many can bring best results.

In the strand of Exploration in our curriculum Te Whāriki, the focus reinforces activity where 'children learn strategies for active exploration, thinking and reasoning", and exploration of space where children are "making sense of the natural, social, physical and material worlds". Water, sand and logs are open ended resources that can be played with and created in different ways and provide opportunities for you to be a creative and critical thinker as you experiment, problem solve and refine your ideas.

HOW DO WE STRETCH AND GROW GIDEON'S LEARNING FURTHER?

One of the goals in Te Whāriki is for children to be encouraged to learn with and alongside others. Our intention is to encourage and scaffold strategies for you Gideon to initiate, maintain and enjoy relationships with others, and as you continue to seek opportunities to interact with others, your relationships will deepen.

Learning Story 8.2 *Collaboration*

Author: Kim Parkinson

EMBRACING A CHALLENGE

Kim

Gideon, over the last few days you have been working on the monkey bars and setting yourself a goal to swing from one end to the other. This morning I joined you in the park and you were keen to show me your progress. Gideon, you stretched out to reach the bars and before I had time to get my camera ready you had reached the second bar before dropping to the ground. "Wow, Gideon, you were so fast I didn't have time to take some photos", I said to you. "Oh, I do it again", you replied, and quickly returned to the top of the red box.

This time I was ready and captured you in action. Gideon, I could see that you had a great strategy of using the momentum from your body to propel you forward as you grasped at the next bar. Gideon, you very quickly made your way to the third bar before dropping to the ground. You continued to practise and practise, each time making it as far as the third bar. Gideon, it was great to see your enthusiasm and can do attitude as you returned over and over again to the monkey bars, and it was only when your hands became a bit tender that you decided to take a rest.

A WEEK LATER: Gideon, it has been a week since you were working on the monkey bars, and this morning Verity was outside when she noticed you swinging along the bars. Just as you had done on your previous attempts on the monkey bars, you tried to reach the next bar. After several more attempts on the bars, you decided to try a new strategy and start from the blue box. Gideon, you gave this a few goes and then decided to return to the red box to start your monkey bar challenge again.

Gideon, you steadied yourself on the red box and grasped the first rung. Swinging your legs, you stretched out for the second bar, then the third, the fourth, the fifth, and finally the very last bar, the sixth bar. Gideon, you had successfully swung from one end of the bars to the other! This was a great achievement, and one you celebrated by returning to the bars and repeating again, in fact three more times! You then decided you would try from the other end of the bars, but after several attempts you decided the red box end was easier. Gideon, this might be a challenge that you could work on now that you have succeeded on the monkey bars from the red box.

A few days later you were back in the park practising again, and Nadine captured you on video. I have made a DVD for you to use as a tool for revisiting and provocation, and I'm sure you will enjoy sharing this with your family. Enjoy!

WHAT LEARNING DO I SEE HAPPENING FOR GIDEON?

Gideon, there have been several stories written about your can do attitude and perseverance as you set goals for your learning and this disposition continues to strengthen as you seek new opportunities and revisit prior experiences. The monkey bars have been a challenge that you have engaged in for some time now and it was exciting to see you making progress as you concentrated on your task and saw this challenge as an opportunity to extend your learning. Gideon, we know that when you take on a challenge it takes time, effort and a willingness to explore possibilities. As you worked on the monkey bars you trialled a new approach as you started from the blue box end of the bars, formulating your own working theories and discovering after several attempts that the red box end was more accessible. We know that practising is an important strategy and you were keen to revisit you experiences, building on the knowledge you have gathered as you mastered the monkey bars. Gideon, you were so pleased with your work and it is this intrinsic motivation, a personal hunger that empowers you and motivates you to succeed.

> 'One's identity as a competent learner and knower is to some extent built around the notion of making progress, getting better at something, becoming more expert and knowing more'.
> Margaret Carr 2008

Learning Story 8.3 *Embracing a challenge*

Author: Kim Parkinson

A Story from Home

Hi Kim, thanks for the lovely update on Gideon's learning experiences at Bush Kindergarten. I appreciate the time and effort the teachers had put into each stage of Gideon's learning journey.

Recently, Gideon was thrown off from a Flying Fox at Keith Hay Park and he was so upset with himself and the Flying Fox. He kept talking about how he would never want to get onto any Flying Fox. Then his monkey bar challenge Learning Story came to my mind. I began asking him how many rungs could he do and he replied proudly, "6". Then I asked again, "How many times did you fall to the ground before you could complete the monkey bar?" And I also reminded him of the blisters he got on his palm but he didn't give up. Two days later, Gideon went back to the same Flying Fox, requesting us to pull him along first though. We asked Gideon if he wanted to do solo, he said he will come back when he is 5 years old! I feel it is this mentally revisiting the experience from the monkey bar challenge that helped him to recover from the Flying Fox failure much quicker than I expected! We are so proud of him.

I had read the BullRush Learning Story on StoryPark to Gideon. A day later, while we were having our family dinner conversations, Gideon shared his experience on BullRush. He said, "When I first played BullRush, I didn't know the rules well. I was tagged. Now I know [the rules], and I ran so fast and nobody can tag me!"

I really enjoy reading Gideon's Learning Stories. I am sure all the Learning Stories in his portfolio would become great memories of how he survived and succeeded each playtime and each game with resilience and a growth mindset.

Dorcus

Learning Story 8.4   *A story from home*
Author: Dorcus Lim

A Caterpillar Design

Karen

Gideon, you have recently completed an abstract mosaic tile design and this was a great introduction to the process required to successfully complete this type of artwork. Today you joined me at the mosaic table and expressed your interest in creating another tile. I suggested a picture design could be your next task as this would stretch your learning and provide the opportunity for you to develop your skills further. Gideon, you set to work to draw a design, and you took time to practise and explore possibilities, your final design was a caterpillar and you decided this was to be the pattern for your tile.

With your design transferred on to the white base tile you set to work on the next step, tiling. I cut the rectangle shapes while you glued them in place. You worked with such efficiency and focus and persisted with the task until the outline was completed. Keen to continue, your next plan was to fill in the caterpillar's body and burgundy was to be your colour of choice. Gideon, you hunted through the basket to find small pieces and glued them in place.

The Next Day...

Today you began work on the background and tiled the tricky part around the caterpillar's legs. We used quite a few long rectangle shapes to fit between the caterpillar's legs and with the fiddly part completed you left your tile to dry.

The Next Week...

Gideon, you returned to the mosaic table today and your intention was to complete the tiling process, you love to get stuck in and you had glue everywhere! I wonder if it was the tactile feeling of the glue that you enjoyed? You ensured there was plenty of glue on each tile and stuck them securely into place. The light purple colour you chose for your background complemented your design and the light colour emphasized your caterpillar, ensuring this was the focal point of your tile.

The Next Week...

Gideon, your tile was now completely dry and you were ready to continue with the next step, cleaning and grouting. This was no ordinary cleaning job but quite a major task as there was a lot of dried glued over every tile. You were not deterred by the task and worked alongside Verity to clean every last bit of glue off your tile. You applied the grout to fill the cracks and when the excess was wiped off your beautiful caterpillar design emerged.

Learning Story 8.5 *A Caterpillar design (part 1)*

Author: Karen Ramsey

What learning do I see happening for Gideon?

Gideon is fast becoming an expert at creating mosaic tile designs and it is great to see him directing this process from start to finish. Dorcas, you shared that "Gideon is very proud of the two mosaic tiles he had created. He even brought it out to show his adult friends. And we went around looking for the right size mini easel stand to display his mosaic art work, specifically on the display area where he can see at eye level and access it anytime". Your insights into Gideon's learning are helpful and you mention that Gideon has many pictures and designs in his mind but he can get 'frustrated' when he can't really put these ideas into a drawing. You have noticed he is confident to use other materials such as folding paper to create a rocket or building with lego and duplo to express ideas. At kindergarten we have noticed when Gideon is painting or drawing he often fills the whole page with one colour and I wonder if this is a strategy he is currently using until he feels ready to begin to embrace the challenge of drawing. I get the feeling that Gideon will have very clear ideas in his mind and his frustration comes from not being able to replicate what he is 'seeing' in his mind. As Gideon's learning journey continues and his growth mindset continues to develop, we will gently encourage him to have a go. An important characteristic of a growth mindset is the view of seeing failure as a pathway to learning and how the learning disposition, persistence and practising will support you to achieve new challenges. We would say, "You can't draw a .... yet but through practising and working hard you will learn to". Dorcas, you shared that Gideon's interest in drawing is developing and recently Gideon has started to express his ideas through drawing lines and patterns. Making a picture tile provided motivation for Gideon to explore an interest in drawing and it is exciting to see Gideon making progress towards this goal.

How will we stretch and strengthen Gideon's learning?
Dorcas, as you have expressed you will continue to work alongside Gideon, and support him to bring his ideas to life through the medium of drawing. Gideon has recently shown an interest in making books and this task provides a meaningful way for Gideon to explore and practise the art of drawing. This type of exploration will also provide the opportunity for Gideon to become comfortable with uncertainty and knowing that it is ok not to be successful on your first attempt but rather this as an important part of the learning process. Dorcas, I look forward to sharing many more conversations with you, as it is through working through a collaborative process that we will strengthen Gideon's learner identity and his disposition to be a highly motivated self-directed learner.

Learning Story 8.5 *A Caterpillar design (part 2)*
Author: Karen Ramsey

On this occasion he makes a caterpillar design (and later he will add a lion design to his collection). It takes him several weeks of occasional work to complete this task, and the Learning Story describes the process in some detail. In Chapter 5 we quoted Elliot Eisner, an artist as well as a creative educator, asking the following question in his book *Reimagining Schools*: 'Are parents helped to understand what their child has accomplished in class?' (Eisner, 2005: 190).

In this account, Learning Stories document the process of tile-making over three productions. In the teacher's commentary about what learning this represents, she includes a comment from his mother: 'Dorcas, you shared: "Gideon is very proud …"'. She adds, 'Your insights into Gideon's learning are helpful and you mention that Gideon has many pictures and designs in his mind but he can get "frustrated" when he can't really put these ideas into a drawing'. She then comments on the possibilities for him, referring to Carol Dweck's mindsets; a page explaining Dweck's mindsets is included in every family's portfolio when their child arrives at the centre. Note that we introduced Carol Dweck's work in Chapter 3.

Concluding comments: purposes, priorities and pitfalls

In this book we have canvassed many ways in which Learning Stories should, are and can be constructed. We have noted purposes, priorities and pitfalls, and we have built Learning Stories around common questions. We started with *purposes*: why Learning Stories? and argued for learning dispositions as a way of 'making learning whole', as David Perkins insists. This then led to some *priorities*: requiring the writers of Learning Stories to 'be formative', to see the story as part of a journey; and to 'be fair', to assess learning dispositions, not just knowledge and skill. The next part of the argument was to have powerful frameworks in mind, to see the Learning Stories as a part of the developing whole, the learner self. We argued that for teachers and learners, ambiguity provokes *possibility thinking*, and uncertainty invites *collaboration, creativity* and *communication*: four useful dispositions for young children and for those who work with them. Perkins has discussed the 'person-plus' that frames Chapter 6, and we like the title of Urie Bronfenbrenner's 2005 book as a link for the chapter entitled 'Developing partnerships with families': *Making Human Beings Human* (Bronfenbrenner, 2005). This book sets out a bioecological perspective on human development, which aims to contribute to 'the design of effective social policies and programmes that can counteract newly emerging, developmentally disruptive influences' (Bronfenbrenner, 2005: 12).

This notion of the parts fitting a whole was raised by Malaguzzi's 'tangle of spaghetti'; perhaps Gideon's mosaic tiles might be seen as a metaphor. We include his caterpillar mosaic again as a final full-stop for this book. It is made up of pieces, some of which are only semi-fitting. This is not entirely an abstract con-struction; there is a picture there; not easily labelled and described. So it is with the learning child. The metaphor breaks down, however, because the parts, and the way in which they fit together over a life-time, shift and change, and the frame becomes considerably expanded. The final chapter, 'A workshop', will include some of the *pitfalls* to consider. One of the major pitfalls that we all will meet is a culture of testing. This is always a stumbling block, and we have suggested a re-framing of 'measuring' in this chapter. We hope the book will provide some ideas for conversations about learning and assessment.

Further thinking

1. What are some of the 'pieces' that contribute to powerful mosaics (in the primary school or early years curriculum that you know best)? Can you describe some examples of the 'pieces' in practice? How are they put together?

Further reading

Carr, Margaret and Lee, Wendy (2012) *Learning Stories: Constructing Learner Identities in Early Education*. London: SAGE. Chapter 6: Appropriating knowledge and learning dispositions in a range of increasingly complex ways.

New Zealand Ministry of Education (2007) *Kei tua o te Pae* Book 14 – *Communication*. Downloadable at: www.education.govt.nz/assets/Documents/ Early-Childhood/Kei-Tua-o-te-Pae/ECEBooklet14Full.pdf (accessed 3 December 2018).

9

A Learning Story Workshop

Assessments in narrative format can offer plotlines that are designed to resonate with other situations and circumstances and to illustrate multiple possible actions and futures. Sociocultural views of learning and assessment enable us to take account of this complexity. (Bronwen Cowie and Margaret Carr, 2016: 396)

Key messages

- Four parts to writing a Learning Story:

    1. Documenting the story of an event
    2. The learning analysis
    3. Planning and responding
    4. Reflection

- Workshop each chapter

Introduction

This chapter sets out frameworks for considering a workshop on writing Learning Stories as a form of assessment. The word 'assessment' comes from a fifteenth-century Old French word *assesser*, which comes from the Latin *assidēre* which means 'to sit beside'. We like this derivation of the word as it applies to Learning Stories. Frequently the child will read and revisit a Learning Story while he or she is *sitting beside* the teacher, carer or parent as they look at the learning portfolio together.

The chapters in this book have provided a rationale for a narrative format for assessment, and presented some of the difficulties. They argued for the development of *learning dispositions* as the pathway for learning (Chapter 3), and that one of the values of Learning Stories is that they are formative – they include suggestions for a way forward (Chapter 2). Chapter 4 (Recognising Powerful Frameworks) insisted that an assessment should have in mind a long-distance aim, and Chapter 5 (Managing Ambiguity) reminded us all that the pathways are uncertain and the meaning of what is observed is often ambiguous. Chapter 6 highlighted the value of sharing the responsibility for learning with the learner; and Chapter 7 argued for developing partnerships with families and the opportunities for Learning Stories to do this. This chapter will introduce some ideas and provocations for a group of teachers to explore together the ideas about learning and assessment in the previous chapters, and, in particular, to try them out in their own practice.

Threaded throughout this chapter is one Learning Story from Vera's portfolio[1]. Vera began at a kindergarten in New Zealand at age three years and two months. Examples of writing the four parts of a Learning Story are taken from a Learning Story written by a teacher when she was four-and-a-half years old.

Writing a Learning Story

1. Documenting the story of an event
2. The learning analysis
3. Planning and responding
4. Reflection

1 Documenting the story of an event

What the teacher observed happening, and/or participated in, and decided to document

We reproduce here (from Chapter 1) the 'progressive filter' of early years' teaching. Of course, over just one day, early years teachers are noticing, recognising and responding to children many, many times. In this chapter, as in the earlier chapters, all people who educate and care for children outside their home are described as teachers.[2]

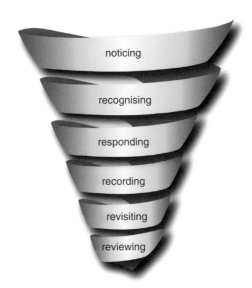

Some of what you *notice* will be *recognised* and given a *response*. That response may be a smile, a frown, a 'thumbs up' or a comment. A few of those noticed, recognised and responded-to events will be noted down or remembered to record as a Learning Story. Sometimes we refer to those moments that we capture as WOW or magic moments. These may be very ordinary events or episodes, but for the particular child they are significant moments or episodes of learning. In some of these moments the ordinary can become extraordinary.

Frequently teachers will take photographs of the children at play and at work. There are ethical considerations here; although rare, some families do not want their children photographed, and when families enrol, any Learning Story programme must be carefully described, illustrated, and permissions must be gained.

If teachers are to recognise moments that matter to the child, teachers will know the children well, recognise that this is a significant moment in the child's learning, and write with the child in mind. A Learning Story will describe where the learning occurred, the context, who was involved and how it began. It may note the role the child played, for example: were they the 'helper and supporter'? Did they offer lots of suggestions? Were they problem-solving for someone else? etc. How did the child participate and what happened next? Sometimes you will want to include exactly what the child said. At other times it will be more general. Watch and listen carefully; write in ways that illustrate some of the learning dispositions you know are important for the children with deep interest, close attention to detail, and (often) a curiosity about what this means for 'where to next'. We suggest that teachers will:

- Start with words such as 'I' and 'learning observed', to show it is your perspective of the learning.
- Think about the audience. It is useful to begin by writing directly to the child. Consider also writing directly to the family.
- Know the children well, read their portfolios, and have some ideas about the appearance of progress, a way forward or a new domain of interest, curiosity and/or challenge.
- Provide a clear focus on the child's strengths, interests and passions.
- Give the Learning Story a title.
- Invite families to share their perspectives on their child's learning.
- Know the curriculum well: the powerful frameworks.
- Possibly take photographs during the day; some of these will become the basis for a Learning Story.

Unlike most school classrooms, early childhood teachers teach and care collaboratively with their peers. Whenever it is possible in their busy daily schedules, it is very helpful for them to meet together with other teachers to talk, and ask each other for advice about recent stories written or in progress.

An example from Vera's Learning Story

Vera's Learning Story: I did it!

It was a Wednesday afternoon, our favourite afternoon of the week ... Bush Kindergarten [an area of bush and trees behind the kindergarten]! I was with a few children at the commando ropes, when Vera, you came and joined us. I know that this is something that you have been practising Vera, so it was great to see you revisiting this learning experience.

You lined up by the tree, patiently waiting for your turn. When your turn came, you expertly climbed up into the tree and then carefully figured out the best way to get your hands and feet on the ropes. Once there, you began to inch your way along. Half way along you dropped down, and went back to the tree to try again.

Up you climbed and began your journey along the rope. I could really see the look of concentration on your face Vera, and you used your core strength to balance and steady yourself when you began to wobble.

Suddenly I noticed that you were nearly at the end! 'Wow Vera! Look how far you have gone!' I commented, and a big smile spread across your face. When you had gone as far to the end as you felt comfortable, you jumped down. 'I did it!' you cried. With your sense of achievement fresh in your mind, you climbed back up the tree and back along the commando rope. Once again you made it to the end and jumped down. 'I did it again!'

Photos 9.1, 9.2 and 9.3

Photos 9.4, 9.5 and 9.6

Photos 9.7, 9.8 and 9.9

Discussion and writing during the workshop

What did you especially notice about this record of the event for Vera? Share your thoughts with the group. Share some stories about events and children, in the context you know best, that you would like to write.

Write the story of one of these events (in preparation for a Learning Story). Imagine what photographs you might include. Remember that the photos will also help tell the story, and in the revisiting phase, it is the photos that enable the children to remember and 'read' their own portfolios and their learning progress. Share the story you write with others. Be critical of yourself and others!

2 The learning analysis

Analysis of the learning changes the 'story' into a Learning Story

The learning analysis makes the connection to the learning. Why was this moment you chose to write about so significant for the child? What excited you about this particular learning moment? Is this something that has been written about before? Use the child's portfolio as a planning tool and see if you can make connections back to the disposition/interests you are writing about in the learning analysis. It is sometimes hard to be definite about what has been 'learnt', so choose your wording carefully. You may have to write, 'I think you were discovering …', or 'It looked like you were interested in the way …'. Talk about the learning strategies the child used – did they seek support, use resources in creative ways, etc. Think about the knowledge and skills and how dispositions such as perseverance, curiosity and sensitivity to the needs of the others supported the child's learning. Explain why what you have documented is so significant – if a child is beginning to play with others; talk about how relationships are important for children. Or, if you are writing about a child's artwork, talk about the complex processes involved. Dig deep – how does this Learning Story connect to other Learning Stories for this child? Discuss why you used particular teaching strategies. It is also important to consider the ways in which you might make your practice and pedagogy visible in the Learning Story. Consider sharing evidence or theoretical ideas supporting your ideas and your thinking. The following graphic illustrates that learning dispositions and the skills and knowledge might be separated is a 'split lens'.

An example from Vera's Learning Story

What learning did I see for Vera?

It was certainly very exciting to see Vera going almost all the way to the very end of the commando ropes! In the Learning Story that [another teacher] wrote, 'Being brave', she talked about practising being a wise strategy for learning. Vera's success and progress in this self-initiated challenge is proof of this.

We are interested in Guy Claxton's work around learning power, which links very closely with the dispositional lens of *Te Whāriki*, our early childhood curriculum. Guy Claxton states: 'Good learners do not grow by being protected from difficulty, but by engaging with it, and thereby developing their stamina and skill' (Claxton, 2002: 79).

Discussion and writing during the workshop

What other learning dispositions did you especially notice? Share your thoughts with the group. Share your favourite learning dispositions for young children: why are these special for you? Are they in your curriculum? What writers might you quote to support your favourites? Discuss with others.

Return to your writing the story of an event (in preparation for a Learning Story) in Part 1 of this workshop. You may already have edited it after the critical discussions during Part 1.

Now add a learning analysis. Refer to the powerful framework (see Chapter 4 in this book) that you know best, but make sure you include learning dispositions as well (see Chapter 3 in this book if they are not easily found in your national curriculum). Share this with others. Be critical of yourself and of others!

3 Planning and responding

Add strengthen, support, complexity, etc. to the learning and foster learning dispositions

This will show some of the 'golden threads' of individual planning. This should relate to the narrative and to the analysis. Think about a child's funds of knowledge and how their wider learning community supports their learning. Think about how to add complexities to the work. Do resources need to be moved or added? How can the continuity of learning be supported? Does the child need more time to further explore this work? The equipment and resources may need to be available for a long time. Do you need to work with the child to find out more about their intentions and discover more about their theories?

An example from Vera's Learning Story

Responding to Vera

Vera it is great to see your willingness to set challenges that require persistence and perseverance to reach your goals going from strength to strength. I can see you using this mindset in other areas of your learning too as you

(Continued)

(Continued)

confidently explore your interests (such as making books). We see you children as planners of your own learning. I wonder what your next plan will be?

Responding to Vera's parents

To Vera's parents (named), I really enjoyed your story from home in relation to Bush Kindergarten. You talk about having seen Vera develop a lot through Bush Kindergarten, and about her becoming more confident in making decisions about what she does on a daily basis. We can see this happening for Vera as well, particularly when it comes to making plans and setting her own goals.

Discussion and writing during the workshop

Return to your writing the story of an event (in preparation for a Learning Story) in Part 1 of this workshop, and the learning analysis that you wrote in Part 2. You may already have edited the learning analysis after the critical discussions during Part 2.

Now write a planning and responding section (writing to the child and to the family). Refer to Chapter 2 (Being Formative), Chapter 6 (Sharing Responsibility with the Learners) and Chapter 7 (Developing Partnerships with Families).

What planning might you suggest? See your analysis. What resources are available in the learning space for children to learn (for instance) perseverance in more than one place? What resources or opportunity would you like to add or change to enable this to happen? Is it possible for children to choose their own challenges? Do families share their perspectives with the teachers? Discuss with others, and think of ways to encourage these developments.

Share this completed Learning Story with others. Be critical of yourself and others!

4 Reflection
Children and teachers reflecting back on the learning

noticing

recognising

responding

recording

revisiting

reviewing

Children enjoy revisiting and reviewing their portfolios, and conversations with their teachers. Such reflections are included in *Learning Stories: Constructing Learner Identities in Early Education* (Carr and Lee, 2012), where children are invited to consider their learning progress further. On pages 44 to 45 of that book, Zeb is having a conversation with his teacher about the photos of a fish project that he and his dad initiated when they brought some fish to the early childhood centre. He is reflecting on that project, and adding new thoughts. A poster of different fish was added to the wall during the project, and that drew comments from Zeb as well. In that book we commented on page 46 that children develop 'islands of expertise' if they are enabled to return to prior events, via photographs and stories, again and again. We quoted Mihaly Csikszentmihalyi, a researcher and writer with a deep interest and curiosity about what makes people creative and we quote him here (differently but on the same page) talking about developing deep interests, following a comment from a historian who described her 'delight' in getting 'really curious about some problem'. Csikszentmihalyi says:

> Without such interest it is difficult to become involved in a domain deeply enough to reach its boundaries and then push them further. (1996: 53)

An example from Vera's Learning Story

Vera did become very interested in persevering with making books, dictating increasingly complex stories that include her favourite characters from traditional stories. Another teacher at the kindergarten wrote in a later Learning Story:

> It is a common sight to see Vera at the drawing table most mornings as she works on her latest ideas for her books. We have noticed Vera's ideas becoming more complex as she shares her work with us, and this morning, when Vera came and asked me to write her story, I reflected on the language she is using and how this has developed over time.

Discussion and writing during the workshop

What do you think might capture the child's interest in the Learning Story you have now written? Imagine what Learning Story you might write next. The portfolio that houses your Learning Stories will illustrate, and comment specifically on, progress over time. See Chapter 8 in this book and the ABCD dimensions of progress in Carr and Lee's *Learning Stories* (2012: 136).

Share your ideas with others.

Further thinking

There are many ways you can workshop this book. The important ideas will be explored and deepened if you also consider your own learning dispositions! The principles that are deeply embedded in this philosophy of assessment are as important for the teacher as they are for children. Are you a curious, engaged, persistent learner who can articulate learning and take responsibility to share your ideas with others? We hope that the chapters in this book will each contribute towards helping you to develop the courage and the language to explore difficult ideas about assessment in dialogue with others. The Further Thinking sections in each chapter are designed to start discussions and to create even further thinking.

Workshop each chapter

Here is a possible framework for a number of workshops, each workshop could be framed around each of the chapters from Chapter 2 through to Chapter 8:

1. Invite all workshop participants to read a specific chapter prior to a workshop with a view to bringing back to the group the ideas that individually excited them and why.
2. Read the Learning Stories in this chapter. Which Learning Stories create the most interest and discussion? Why was this? How does the discussion further the teachers' thinking and capacity for critique?
3. Tackle the Further Thinking section at the end of each chapter and share ideas.
4. Encourage the participants to bring a Learning Story that they have developed that is relevant to the chapter. Teachers and interested educators and carers strengthen their practice by sharing examples from their own contexts, and by reading their Learning Stories to others.
5. Explore one or more of the follow-up readings from the Further Reading section at the end of each chapter.
6. Explore one or more of the seven strands to the 'tangle' of communication expertise in Chapter 8.
    i.   Choose your favourite, and share links with others to an example of this strand from your own personal learning journey.
    ii. Describe an example of children's learning that is familiar to you. What was the role of the teacher and the resources in this example? Write and discuss a Learning Story that could have been written about this.

Final comment

We encourage you all to write Learning Stories that make a difference. Many children will revisit and review their learning portfolios throughout their lifetime, keeping alive the memories of resilience, courage, collaboration, kindness and other positive dispositions. A portfolio illustrates real events that began to construct life-long learning dispositions, reminding them of this over the years as they grow and develop further as learners. Remember the privilege it is to touch children's learning lives in this way and appreciate that this not only traces the professional quality of an early years experience, but it also traces the construction of powerful learning and teaching.

Photo 9.10 *Esther Gloree sharing her early childhood portfolio with her brother and Kindergarten teacher, Karen Ramsay, on her 21st birthday*

Notes

1. See Carr, M., Lee, W., Ramsey, K., Parkinson, K., Priebs, N. Brown, V. (2019) Te Whāriki, Learning Stories and Possibility Thinking: Tracking the Progress. In A. Gunn, & J. Nuttall (eds) Weaving Te Whāriki (3rd Edition). Wellington: NZCER Press for more detail on Vera's portfolio of Learning Stories.

2. We reproduce here (from Chapter 1) the 'progressive filter' of early years' teaching. Of course, over just one day, early years teachers are noticing, recognising and responding to children many, many times. In this chapter, as in the earlier chapters, all people who educate and care for children outside their home are described as teachers.

Bibliography

Assessment Reform Group (1998) *Inside the Black Box: Raising Standards Through Classroom Assessment*. Cambridge: University of Cambridge.

Assessment Reform Group (1999) *Assessment for Learning: Beyond the Black Box*. Cambridge: University of Cambridge.

Assessment Reform Group (2002) *Testing, Motivation and Learning*. Cambridge: University of Cambridge.

Assessment Reform Group (2007) *Information and Communication Technology Inside the Black Box*. Cambridge: University of Cambridge.

Assessment Reform Group (2009) *Inside the Primary Black Box*. Cambridge: University of Cambridge.

Bell, B. and Cowie, C. (2001) *Formative Assessment and Science Education*. Dordrecht, Boston and London: Kluwer.

Black, P., Harrison, C., Lee, C., Marshall, B. and Wiliam, D. (2002) *Working Inside the Black Box: Assessment for Learning in the Classroom*. London: nferNelson.

Black, P., Harrison, C., Lee, C., Marshall, B. and Wiliam, D. (2003) *Assessment for Learning: Putting it into Practice*. Maidenhead: Open University Press.

Bronfenbrenner, U. (ed.) (2005) *Making Human Beings Human: Bioecological Perspectives on Human Development*. Thousand Oaks, CA: SAGE.

Brooker, L., Blaize, M., Edwards, S. (2014) The SAGE Handbook of Play and Learning in Early Childhood. London: SAGE.

Brown, S. (2009) *Play: How it shapes the brain, opens the imagination, and invigorates the soul*. Carlton North, Victoria, Australia 3054: Scribe Publications.

Bruner, J. (1986) *Actual Minds, Possible Worlds*. Cambridge, MA and London: Harvard University Press.

Bruner, J. (2003) *Making Stories*. Cambridge, MA: Harvard University Press.

Cagliari, P., Castagnetti, M., Giudici, C., Rinaldi, C., Vecchi, V. and Moss, P. (2016) *Loris Malaguzzi and the Schools of Reggio Emilia: A Selection of His Writings and Speeches, 1945–1993*. London: Routledge.

Carr, M. (2001) *Assessment in Early Childhood Settings: Learning Stories*. London: SAGE.

Carr, M. and Claxton, G. (1989) The costs of calculation. *New Zealand Journal of Educational Studies, 24* (2): 129–140.

Carr, M. and Lee, W. (2012) *Learning Stories: Constructing Learner Identities in Early Education*. London: SAGE.

Carr, M., Ramsey, K., Parkinson, K., Priebs, N. and Brown, V. (2019) Te Whāriki, Learning Stories and Possibility Thinking: Tracking the Progress. In A. Gunn, & J. Nuttall (eds) Weaving Te Whāriki (3rd Edition). Wellington: NZCER Press (in press).

Clarkin-Phillips, J. and Carr, M. (2014) An affordance network for engagement: increasing parent and family agency in an early childhood education setting. *European Early Childhood Education Journal, 20* (2): 177–187.

Claxton, G. (1990) *Teaching to Learn: A Direction for Education*. London: Cassell.

Claxton, G. (2002) *Building Learning Power: Helping Young People Become Better Learners*. Bristol: TLO Limited.

Claxton, G. (2004) Learning is learnable (and we ought to teach it). In S. J. Cassell (ed.), *Ten Years On Report*. Bristol: National Commission for Education, pp. 237–250.

Claxton, G., Chambers, M., Powell, G. and Lucas, B. (2011) *The Learning Powered School*. Bristol: TLO Ltd.

Claxton, G. (2018) *The Learning Power Approach: Teaching Learners to Teach Themselves*. Thousand Oaks, California: Corwin.

Collins English Dictionary, 3rd Edition (1992). Glasgow: Harper/Collins.

Cowie, B. and Carr, M. (2016) Narrative assessments: a sociocultural view. In M. A. Peters (ed.), *Encyclopedia of Educational Philosophy and Theory*. Singapore: Springer, pp. 396–4001.

Craft, A. (2005) *Creativity in Schools: Tensions and Dilemmas*. London and New York: Routledge.

Craft, A. (2013) Childhood, possibility thinking and wise, humanising educational futures. *International Journal of Educational Research*, *61*: 126–134.

Csikszentmihalyi, M. (1993) *The Evolving Self*. New York: Harper Collins.

Csikszentmihalyi, M. (1996) *Creativity, Flow and the Psychology of Discovery and Invention*. New York: Harper Collins.

Csikszentmihalyi, M. (1997) *Finding Flow: The Psychology of Engagement with Everyday Life*. New York: Harper Collins.

Davis, K., Wright, J., Carr, M. and Peters, S. (2013) *Key Competencies, Assessment and Learning Stories: Talking with Teachers and Students. Workbook and DVD*. Wellington: NZCER Press.

Drummond, M. J. (1993, 2003, 2012) *Assessing Children's Learning*. Abingdon, Oxon: Routledge.

Dweck, C. S. (2006) *Mindset*. New York: Random House.

Edwards, C. P. and Rinaldi, C. (eds.). (2009) *The Diary of Laura: Perspectives on a Reggio Emilia diary*. Redleaf Press.

Eisner, E. W. (2005) *Reimagining Schools: The Selected Works of Elliot W. Eisner*. London and New York: Routledge.

Feldman, C. and Wertsch, J. (1976) Context dependent properties of teachers' speech. In *Youth and Society*, *8*: 227–258.

Gonzàlez, N., Moll, L. C. and Armanti, C. (2005) *Funds of Knowledge: Theorizing Practice in Households, Communities and Classrooms*. Mahwa, NJ: Laurence Erlbaum Associates.

Goodman, N. and Cherrington, S. (2015) Parent, whānau, and teacher engagement through online portfolios in early childhood education. *Early Childhood Folio*, *19* (1): 10–16.

Gopnik, A. (2010) *The Philosophical Baby: What children's minds tells us about truth, love and the meaning of life*. New York: Picador.

Greeno, J. G. and Gresalfi, M. S. (2008) Opportunities to learn in practice and identity. In P. A. Moss, D. C. Pullin, J. P. Gee, E. H. Haertal and L. J. Young (eds), *Assessment, Equity, and Opportunity to Learn*. Cambridge and New York: Cambridge University Press.

Gresalfi, M. S. (2009) Taking up opportunities to learn: constructing dispositions in mathematics classrooms. *Journal of the Learning Sciences*, *18*: 327–369.

Gunn, A. and Nuttall, J. (2019) *Weaving Te Whāriki* (3rd edn). Wellington: NZCER Press.

Hartley, C., Rogers, P., Smith, J., Peters, S. and Carr, M. (2012) *Crossing the Border: A Community Negotiates the Transition from Early Childhood to Primary School*. Wellington: NZCER Press.

Haste, H. (2004) Constructing the citizen. *Political Psychology*, *25* (3): 413–439.

Haste, H. (2008) Good thinking: the creative and competent mind. In A. Craft, H. Gardner and G. Claxton (eds), *Creativity, Wisdom, and Trusteeship: Exploring the Role of Education*. Thousand Oaks, CA: Corwin Press, pp. 96–104.

Hattie, J. (2009) *Visible Learning*. Routledge: London.

Hattie, J. and Yates, G. (2014) *Visible Learning and the Science of How We Learn*. Abingdon, Oxon: Routledge.

Holloway, B. (2018) Play: a secondary concern? *SET: Research Information for Teachers, Special Issue: Learning Through Play and Games*. NZCER Press. DOI: https://doi.org/10.18296/set.0116.

Hooker, T. (2015) Assessment for learning: a comparative study of paper-based portfolios and on-line ePortfolios. *Early Childhood Folio, 19* (1): 17–24.

Huber, J., Caine, V., Huber, M. and Steeves, P. (2016) Narrative inquiry as pedagogy in education: the extraordinary potential of living, telling, retelling and reliving stories of experience. *Review of Research in Education, 37* (1): 212–242.

Immordino-Yang, M. H. (2018) *Emotions, Learning, and the Brain: Exploring the Educational Implications of Affective Neuroscience*. New York and London: W.W. Norton and Company.

Kardaras, N. (2016) *Glow Kids – How Screen Addiction Is Hijacking Our Kids – and How to Break the Trance*. New York: St Martin's Press.

Lee, W., Carr, M., Soutar, B. and Mitchell, L. (2013) *Understanding the Te Whāriki Approach: Early Years Education in Practice*. London and New York: Routledge.

Meier, D. (1995) *The Power of Their Ideas: Lessons for America from a Small School in Harlem*. Boston: Beacon Press.

Meier, D. (2002) *In Schools We Trust: Creating Communities of Learning in an Era of Testing and Standardisation*. Boston: Beacon Press.

Mercer, M. and Littleton, K. (2007) *Dialogue and the Development of Children's Thinking: a sociocultural approach*. London and New York: Routledge.

Moll, L. C., Armanti, C., Neff, D. and Gonzàlez, N. (1992) Funds of knowledge for teaching: using a qualitative approach to connect homes and classrooms. *Theory into Practice, 31* (2): 132–141.

Morton, S. M. B., Atatoa Carr, P. E., Bandara, D. K., Grant, C. C., Ivory, V. C., Kingi, T. R., Liang, R., Perese, L. M., Peterson, E., Pryor, J. E., Reese, E., Robinson, R. M., Schmidt, J. M. and Waldie, K. E. (2010) *Growing Up in New Zealand: Before We Are Born*, Report 1. A longitudinal study of New Zealand children and their families. Auckland: Growing Up in New Zealand.

Moss, P., Pullin, D. C., Gee, J. P., Haertel, E. H. and Young, L. J. (eds) (2008) *Assessment, Equity, and Opportunity to Learn*. Cambridge and New York: Cambridge University Press.

New Zealand Ministry of Education (2004a) *Kei Tua o te Pae*. Assessment for Learning: Early Childhood Exemplars. Downloadable at: www.education.govt.nz/early-childhood/teaching-and-learning/assessment-for-learning/kei-tua-o-te-pae-2/ (accessed 3 December 2018).

New Zealand Ministry of Education (2004b) *Kei tua o te Pae Book 1 – An Introduction to Kei Tua o te Pae: He Whakamōhiotanga ki Kei Tua o te Pae*. Wellington: Learning Media. Downloadable at: www.education.govt.nz/assets/Documents/Early-Childhood/Kei-Tua-o-te-Pae/ECEBooklet1Full.pdf (accessed 3 December 2018).

New Zealand Ministry of Education (2004c) *Kei Tua o te Pae Book 2 – Sociocultural Assessment: He Aromatawai Ahurea Pāpori*. Wellington: Learning Media. Downloadable at: www.education.govt.nz/assets/Documents/Early-Childhood/Kei-Tua-o-te-Pae/ECEBooklet2Full.pdf (accessed 3 December 2018).

New Zealand Ministry of Education (2009) *Te Whatu Pōkeka: Kaupapa Māori*. Assessment for Learning: Early Childhood Exemplars. Wellington: Learning Media.

New Zealand Ministry of Education (2017) *Te Whāriki. He whāriki mātauranga mō ngā mokopuna o Aotearoa: Early Childhood Curriculum*.Downloadable at: www.education. govt.nz/assets/Documents/Early-Childhood/Te-Whariki-Early-Childhood-Curriculum-ENG-Web.pdf (accessed 3 December 2018).

Noddings, N. (2003) *Happiness and Education*. New York: Cambridge University Press.

Paley, V. (1988) *Bad Guys Don't Have Birthdays: Fantasy Play at Four*. Chicago and London: University of Chicago Press.

Paley, V. (1990) *The Boy Who Would Be a Helicopter*. Cambridge, MA: Harvard University Press.

Paley, V. (2004) *A Child's Work: The Importance of Fantasy Play*. Chicago, IL: University of Chicago Press.

Paley, V. G. (1997). *The Girl With the Brown Crayon: How children use stories to shape their lives*. Harvard University Press.

Perkins, D. N. (2009a) *Making Learning Whole*. San Francisco, CA: Jossey-Bass.

Perkins D. N. (2009b) Person-plus: a distributed view of thinking and learning. In G. Salomon (ed.), *Distributed Cognitions: Psychological and Educational Considerations*. Cambridge: Cambridge University Press, pp. 88–110.

Perkins, D. N., Jay, E. and Tishman, S. (1993) Beyond abilities: a dispositional theory of thinking. *Merrill-Palmer Quarterly, 39* (1): 1–21.

Peters, S., Hartley, C., Rogers, P., Smith, J. and Carr, M. (2009) Early childhood portfolios as a tool for enhancing learning during the transition to school. *International Journal of Transition to School, 3*: 4–15.

Quintero, E. P. (2015) *Storying learning in early childhood: When children lead participatory curriculum design, implementation, and assessment*. Peter Lang.

Ramsey, K., Breen, J., Sturm, J., Lee, W. and Carr, M. (2006) Roskill South Kindergarten Centre of Innovation 2003–2006, unpublished Final Research Report. University of Waikato, Wilf Malcolm Institute of Educational Research.

Reese, E., Suggate, S., Long, J. and Schaughency, E. (2010) Children's oral narrative and reading skills in the first three years of instruction. *Reading and Writing: An Interdisciplinary Journal, 23* (6): 627–644.

Reese, E., Gunn, A., Bateman, A. and Carr, M. (2019) Teacher-child talk about learning stories in New Zealand: a strategy for eliciting children's complex language. *Early Years: An international research journal* (in press).

Resnick, L. B. (1987) *Education and Learning to Think*. Washington, DC: National Academy Press.

Rinaldi, C. (2006) *In Dialogue with Reggio Emilia: Listening, Researching and Learning*. London and New York: Routledge.

Robinson, K. and Aronica, L. (2009) *The Element: How Finding your Passion Changes Everything*. London: England Penguin.

Rychen, D. S. and Salganik, L. H. (eds) (2003) *Key Competencies for a Successful Life and a Well-Functioning Society*. Cambridge, MA and Gottingen, Germany: Hogrefe and Huber Publishers.

Steele, L. (2007) Accessible porfolios: Making it happen in my centre: An Action Research Study. Unpublished Masters thesis. Wellington: Victoria University of Education.

Stobart, G. (2008) *Testing Times: The Uses and Abuses of Assessment*. London: Routledge.

Stobart, G. (2014) *The Expert Learner*. London: McGraw-Hill Education/Open University Press.

Wenger, E. (1998) *Communities of Practice: Learning, Meaning and Identity*. Cambridge: Cambridge University Press.

Index